A GOOD DAUGHTER

The Story Of
A Mother's Death From Cancer

KATHRYN
HOLMQUIST

Raven Arts Press

A Good Daughter
is first published in 1991 by
The Raven Arts Press
P.O. Box 1430
Finglas
Dublin 11
Ireland

ISBN 1 85186 091 6

The Raven Arts Press receives financial assistance from the Arts Council
(An Chomhairle Ealaíon), Dublin, Ireland.

Design by Dermot Bolger & Susanne Linde. Cover design by Rapid
Productions. Printed and bound in Ireland by Colour Books Ltd,
Baldoyle, Ireland.

January, 1976

I was nineteen years old when I sat on the bench outside his door and waited to be called. Would he take me? Would he like me? All my life I had been working towards the audition I was about to perform and I wrung my hands like a nervous bride. Being a musician was the most important part of my life and I had spent my childhood practising for hours every day. My mother had brought me to the best teachers, paying more than she could afford for lessons. When I remember my childhood, I remember the darkening winter hours between four and six in the afternoon when I would be immersed with my teacher in Brahms, Mozart, Prokofiev, the music filling us with its heat and glory. I remember learning new music, my mind eager to absorb the black notes on the white page, my hands working the music like clay, mixing it, forming it, transforming it. I remember feeling the miraculous union of mind and hands as I sucked the music up as powerfully as whales inhale water. And how I spurted out joyful arcs of Mozart like it was part of me. I never thought about my mother during these magic hours when she sat patiently in her car outside my teacher's house, trying to keep warm, her face dim in the pale cast of the street lamps as she listened to the car radio.

I recalled those lessons as I sat and waited for him outside his studio on the third floor of the conservatory. My bench was on a balcony which looked down on the conservatory's four-storey entrance hall, a grand atrium made of glass. The huge, clear panes were supported by a spiny web of white concrete shaped in a continuous pattern of narrow Gothic arches. The blizzard had begun early that morning and looking out through the glass, I had to squint to protect my eyes from the hot glare of pristine ice which reflected into the building, bathing me in a cold, cathedral light.

This was the building in which I would spend the next four

5

years of my life, studying music theory and composition and, above all, practising. I had been accepted to study at the conservatory several months before. The school accepted only one out of each one hundred pianists who auditioned, so just being there was the greatest accomplishment of my life. But the most important question, still to be resolved, was whether or not I would be accepted by the Professor, who rarely took freshmen into his studio. If he did not accept me, I would have to study with one of the lesser teachers, probably one of the Professor's own students, who took the freshman class. If he accepted me, I would be special, set apart from the other students and I would have a chance of becoming a solo artist.

I shifted on the bench, straightening my back, which hurt out of anxiety. The space above my eyes hurt, too, from wincing against the sunlight. I was scared. Not only was I about to do the most important audition of my life, but afterwards I would be separated from my parents for the first time. The day before, my parents and I had driven together many hundreds of miles from home to the conservatory. We had moved my clothes, music and books into the house I would share with some other students. I had watched my parents paying the tuition, my heart twisting with guilt as my mother wrote the cheque in the bursar's office, each zero a symbol of years of sacrifice. I had a scholarship, but it still wasn't enough.

Now my parents sat waiting outside in their car as they had for so many years. They hadn't wanted to leave me in suspense at the conservatory and, like me, were hoping that I would be accepted by the Professor. I opened my leather music case, pulled out a hairbrush and quickly stroked it through my long, blonde hair. At a piano competition in which I had placed second, I had noticed that the girl who came first was wearing black and white: white blouse, black cardigan, black skirt and a black velvet band in her hair. So I had carefully dressed like her, in undertaker colours.

"Miss Holmquist?"

I shook involuntarily and stood. My hands were wet.

"That's me." I stood and faced him as he poked his head out of his studio. Then he waved me in with his smoking hand, the cigarette ash flickering to the ground.

He was tall, broad and blond. As I passed by him, I smelled coffee and porridge on his breath, mixed with that strangely smelling tobacco smoke that would forever remind me of him. Without thinking or having to be asked, I walked over to the piano, sat on the bench and faced the keyboard, preparing to be asked to play. I'm sure I must have looked like I was about to be shot. What would be his first demand? Bach, probably. Arpeggios? I hoped he wouldn't ask for them in too difficult a key. My hands felt weak.

"Cigarette?" he asked, walking towards me and proffering one from a foreign-looking blue paper box, decorated with a wisp of white smoke that echoed his own breath. I had never been offered a cigarette by an adult before, only by girlfriends who hid them in their schoolbags.

"No thanks."

"You sure?"

"Yea."

"Don't smoke?"

"No.

He seemed surprised that I didn't smoke. It was like he was inviting me to move up onto his level and I was childishly refusing to budge, afraid of the height. I had never been on equal terms with a teacher and the Professor was not merely a teacher, he was a genius and a concert artist whose records I had listened to over and over again.

He crossed the room to his desk and I noticed how big he was. He stood peering down at a letter lying on the desk, without touching it. I looked at his hands as they hung by his sides, half-closed like claws, and saw that they were thick and stocky like mine; not the long, slim fingers pianists are supposed to have.

He saw me looking.

"Let me see your span."

I held up my hand, my palm facing towards him, and spread my thumb and little finger as far apart as I could.

"Jesus, that's twelve notes. I've got twelve notes," he said.

He held up his hand and stretched it wide. Splaying his wide fingers, he held his hand up to mine. We were quiet for a moment, palm against palm, his hand hot and dry, mine cold and damp. I wondered if he noticed that I was trying to keep

7

my hand from shaking.

"Mine's just that little bit wider," he said. "Let me see, how many notes can you get?"

I stretched my fingers out on the keyboard as far as I could.

"Only eleven," he said, satisfied, and continued his interrogation. "You're Susan's student. How long have you been with her?"

"Six years."

"I spoke to her about you last night."

What did they speak about? I wondered.

"Why did she send you to me?" he demanded.

Didn't he know? Wasn't it obvious? I sat with my mouth half-open trying to think of something to say.

"Why me and not somebody else?" he prompted.

"Susan told me you're the best."

"What do you want to learn from me?" he asked, sullen now.

"To be the best musician I can be," I told him, thinking instantly that it was a stupid thing to say. I should be mentioning something more specific, I thought.

"Susan says I have lots of passion in my playing, but that I don't care enough about technique," I added.

He laughed. "Screw technique. Play."

"What will I play?"

"Anything. Know any jazz?"

I stared at my hands, flustered. Jazz? My training had been rigidly classical.

"Go on," he pushed.

"I don't know any jazz," I said, ashamed.

"Okay, Mozart."

"Which Mozart?"

"Any Mozart."

So I started on a sonata. After a few measures, he sat to my left on the piano bench and started playing a jazz riff on the bass notes. I smelled coffee and smoke.

"Get into the beat," he said.

I tried, pathetically, out of my element and awkward in his.

"You've got to play Mozart like jazz. You're too stiff," he said. My hands bumbled over the keys and I felt my face flush red. He played like a demon, turning the once-orderly Mozart into a whirling blur like a ship spinning in a vortex. His presence beside me was oppressive and my arms went stiff.

"Okay, okay." He gave up. "Play me something else. Anything you like."

I felt humiliated. I had to show him. So while I played the Scriabin, then the Brahms, I kept thinking about jazz and I let myself push the music further and harder than I ever had before, letting it carry me over its tall swells.

Twenty minutes later, I dashed down the stairs of the conservatory and outside to my parents, who were waiting in their car.

"He accepted me," I shouted.

"That's wonderful," my mother said,

"Congratulations," said my dad.

"We knew you'd do it," my mother said.

And that was that. None of us smiled. We were too sad. We were going to have to say goodbye. My parents got out of the car and we stood in snow and made our parting, our words turning to frozen clouds in the air. They were going to leave me there at the icy steps of the conservatory to start my independent life. I could see how terribly aware they felt of letting me go, cutting me loose into the world for the first time. I could see my mother trying not to cry as I swallowed my own warm, dense drops in the back of my throat.

"What is he like?" my mother asked suspiciously.

"He's great," I said.

"Can we meet him?" she asked.

The thought of having to approach his door again and introduce my parents terrified me. What would he think?

"I don't think so, he seemed really busy," I told her.

She looked worried. "We don't know anything about him."

"He's the best, Mom. What more do you need to know? Susan wants me to study with him."

"Okay," my mother said, sighing and dropping her shoulders as she did when she felt defeated. Then she squinched up her nose and eyes and turned her face away.

I put my arms around her and hugged her to stave off the tears. She cried, anyway, and pushed me away. Dad embraced me lightly and whispered solemnly, "Take care of yourself."

"Don't worry," I reassured them, trying to sound casually

confident but instantly realising that I probably sounded dismissive instead. As usual, I was trying to seem grown-up by showing them my strongest side.

"Of course you'll be okay," my mother said, forcing herself to smile. "I believe in you."

She always had believed in me and helped me to make the most of my chances and now this was my time to make it work and to show her that I could succeed on my own. My desire to succeed only slightly outweighed my terror at being left to cope alone for the first time in my life.

"Are you sure you have everything you need?" she asked again.

"Will you be warm enough? Do you need anything for your room?"

Any chore or errand could make the parting last longer. She wanted me to collude with her in one last motherly task.

"Don't cry, Mom. I'll be home for the vacation in a few months."

"That's right. The time will fly by," my mother said, comforting herself more than me.

I put my arms around her again with that familiar mix of warmth and diffidence that flavours a daughter's embrace when she believes there will be many more.

As I watched them drive away in the blue stationwagon, I wanted to shout, "don't go." My mother, as though she heard me, turned around and looked at me one last time with her sad face.

My tears flowed as I watched the car move away. My father was driving much more slowly than he usually did, out of respect for the moment. As the car crunched snow, turned a corner and disappeared, carrying away my mother, how was I to know that nothing would ever be the same again between us and that never as long as my mother lived would we embrace again as we did at that first, crucial parting?

★ ★ ★

The Professor was an impatient teacher. My one-hour lessons with him twice each week were packed with both praise and criticism but little practical advice and he seemed to expect me to learn from him by osmosis, as though his mere presence was enough. I took the required classes in music theory and music history but spent most of my time in an eight foot by ten foot room with a piano. The other students were so competitive that social life didn't seem to exist.

For many hours each day I practised the pieces that the Professor assigned but I wasn't getting anywhere. I missed the careful guidance of my teacher at home. At each lesson with the Professor, I hoped to impress him with how much I had bent my performance to his will since the previous lesson but he never seemed to remember which aspects he had directed me to master the previous week.

He always seemed more interested in talking but our conversations were one-sided. I was too shy to respond naturally or to volunteer any subject of conversation.

During the eighth week, I sat outside his studio on the bench as usual, waiting to be called. His door opened and I heard him laughing with a male student. I envied their easy cameraderie. The Professor usually just stared at me, his lips smoking and parting only to make elliptical statements.

That day, after he called me in, he asked me not to sit at the piano, but on a couch near his desk. He made a fuss of going over my file. As my piano professor, he was also my faculty advisor and he was supposed to make sure that things were going smoothly for me.

He asked me about my classes and then, looking at me curiously, he demanded, "are you dating anyone?"

"No."

"I don't believe that."

"It's true."

"What about me then?"

What did he mean? I said nothing.

"Do you think I'm too old?" He made a sorry face.

Not wanting to insult him, I said, "no, you're not too old."

How old was he? Thirty-five? Forty? I wasn't sure.

"I would be very upset if I found out that you were dating anyone other than me," he said.

My mind flew. He was married. He was older. I wasn't attracted to him. He was my teacher. I felt dizzy and sick and couldn't believe what I saw in his face: the single-minded greed. The blank eyes staring through me. The hate-lust. The betrayal.

When it was over, I wanted to die. In a sense, I did. It is difficult to describe how it felt to suddenly discover deep inside an emptiness where once there had been my self. It was like being abruptly bottomed out as though the base of my being was too weak to hold against the pressure bearing down on it so that suddenly I had burst and my essence had drained out leaving me utterly dissipated. One moment, I was a self-contained individual with secret, sacred places where no one had ever intruded and the next moment, I felt empty and trodden upon, like the ballroom after the dance, its chairs askew and bits of trash and other matter littering the dirty floor.

From that angle, of the floor, the world looked distorted.

The black piano legs rose up like trees.

"I like to think of my piano as a great bull," he once said.

What was he thinking of when he said that? I had asked myself when I first heard him say it.

Afterwards, I knew too much about him. His strange behaviour fell into place, bringing a sudden insight which came too late.

I struggled away from him. Grabbed my things. Found the door. Asked him, again, to unlock it. Then I walked out of the room and out of my life. I became, in a moment, someone different with a secret I could not tell.

I walked a short distance until my knees, with surprising predictability, grew weak, then I sat down on a bench in the park, watching the activity on the main street with the sensation that I was distanced from it. I could have been watching a film. I saw him drive along the street in his car and park it nearly opposite. He walked into the sweet shop. In the shadows beyond the shopfront glass, I saw him smiling and talking to the girl who sold chocolates. I saw the girl dip and rise as she gathered a chocolate, put it in the box, dipped to gather another, rose to put it in the box. I watched her rhythm until the box was, apparently, filled. When she stopped, I saw him motion with his hand as though to say: "A few more." Finally, she gave him the box and he gave her some money. A simple transaction. I watched him leave the shop and thought, "how strange. He's buying sweets for his children." It hadn't occured to me before that one could conduct so two very different transactions within the same morning. I expected to see him get into his car and drive away. Instead, he came loping towards me.

I wanted to stand up and run but I couldn't. (I have so many dreams like that in which I am being chased but my legs will not move and my voice will not scream.)

"No one needs to know," he said, smiling at me with an expression which I took to be an imitation of tenderness.

"If they did find out, you know you would have to leave the conservatory."

Who would I dare tell? People knowing would be worse than what had happened.

"You like chocolate, don't you?" he said, handing me the box.

"Thanks," I said, stupidly.

"Smile like a pretty girl," he commanded.

I smiled.

"Will I see you tomorrow?" he asked.

He seemed so off-hand that I was soon able to convince myself that nothing had happened. It was just one of those silly things that occurred between men and women, like a scene in a film, and certainly not to be taken seriously. He was attracted to me, that was all. He did what men do when they're attracted to women. I must have done something to make him think I was interested. I would make sure it never happened again. What was so wrong? Someday I would look back on it and laugh at my own innocence. Reasoning away my feelings like that, I bit into a chocolate and settled into my new self, warily.

13

Childhood

When I was small, my mother used to amuse me by listing all the men she could have married. Earnest Swedish boys who grew up to be bank presidents and the chairmen of multinational corporations. Each had dropped to one knee for my mother and pleaded, "Will you marry me, Ardis?" even before they asked for a kiss. I mused over this while I munched cold cereal at the kitchen table. I imagined my mother dressed like a nineteen-forties movie star in a pale pink chiffon ballgown with a strapless, draped bodice and tight waist with her curly, auburn hair falling over her bare shoulders. I imagined the boys in their formal, black suits and bowties lining up to ask my mother to dance. She chose the handsomest boy and they glided off across the floor looking just like the tiny, child-faced bride and groom that my mother had saved from her wedding cake and kept on a high shelf in the pantry wrapped in tissue paper. To choose a man was to choose a destiny as solid as that. My mother had married for love. Falling in love meant wanting to give the other person everything that you had to give, she told me. So I grew to think of myself like that, as a treasure waiting to be given.

My mother had grown up a pastor's daughter and when she fell in love, she gave herself to become a pastor's wife. When I stood beside my mother in church, we were complete in our place in the front pew. Dressed in her Sunday clothes, my mother always smelled warm and spicy. She wore a black, linen dress with sleeves that stopped just below her elbows and long, white elbow-length gloves. She wore a pillbox hat, also black, with a short black net veil. She was so elegant. I loved to watch her dress beginning with her underclothes, fine wisps of womanhood. Her white lace slip and underneath that a white bra and that uncomfortable girdle that made red marks around her waist and kept her solid. My aunt had alluded to the discomfort of the garment on the way home from church one day.

15

"Let's get home and get these girdles off," she half-whispered, half-giggled wickedly as she sat beside my mother in the back seat of the car. Suddenly they were the pastor's daughters again, tempted by rebellion.

My mother hid her suntanned legs with equally troublesome suntan-coloured stockings, purchased from a special counter in the department store and wrapped in a sturdy pink box. They were private things then to be acquired discreetly, not as they are now, in large, brazen displays in supermarkets.

My mother's stockings snagged and ran so easily that she had to wear special white, nylon mitts when she put them on and when she washed them. I still have them. They remind me of the sweet-and-sour smell of those suntan-coloured stockings and how she kept them in a pink, silk envelope, embroidered with tiny flowers. What a pity no one can wear such a pretty thing, I thought, and I would try the satin envelope on my head as a cap, then model it as a purse as I paraded before my mother's full-length mirror, her stockings scattered on the floor under my feet.

In my place in the front pew, I looked down on my mother's black leather shoes with their stiletto heels. From that angle, her feet were shiny black triangles that carried the imprint of her toes. Cut low, the shoes revealed the tiny slit between her big toe and the smaller one beside it. As I remember them, their black tips point straight towards the kneeling bench at the base of the pew.

I tried to stand as straight and still as my mother. I gave my face its most pious expression and thought of myself as a prim, pilgrim girl, dressed in grey, my disciplined body a symbol of faith. But as the organ music ploughed triumphantly ahead, I let my imagination wander to the scenes I created from ballets and grand spectacles in which I was the lead dancer. I had wanted to be a ballerina ever since my mother brought me to see the Nutcracker Suite.

"Ballet or piano," my mother told me. "Piano is better," she added, "ballet gives you thick legs."

So I danced in my imagination when I was falling asleep at night and on Sunday mornings when I listened to the turgid organ music. As I dreamed, my mother suddenly nudged me with her elbow and gave me that subtle glimpse of disapproval so small that only I could see it. I roused myself from my imagination and caught myself akimbo, my hip slung to the right against the pew like Rousseau's nut-brown native girl, holding her basket. (When my mother brought me to the National Gallery in Washington, D.C. on Sunday afternoons, I always made straight for Rousseau's wildly coloured tropical dreams.) Looking down, I saw one white knee-stockinged leg, its foot twisted casually in its black patent leather shoe, leaning against the kneeling bench. I straightened myself up, uncreased my folds and returned to being the pilgrim girl for as long as I could bear it, keeping myself going by thinking about the impression I must be making. The pilgrim girl wore undergarments so stiff that they made her stand as straight as a cardboard doll.

I hated my dress. It was cream-coloured linen with geometric black embroidery trimming the waistband, the hem of the full skirt and the short, straight sleeves. We were sensible in black-and-white, my mother and I.

I wanted fancy dresses, especially for Easter Sunday. When I was small, my mother and I would buy two new dresses every Easter, one for her and one for me. We would wear them nearly every Sunday until the following autumn. But when the steel mill closed and so many men in the church were laid off, the Easter dresses stopped. It wasn't right for us to show-off new dresses on Easter Sunday when many of the parishioners couldn't afford new clothes, she said. When the flush of Easter had passed, my mother would buy me that one new Sunday dress, knowing that its newness in the front pew would not be noticed quite as much.

I sort of understood, but my dress felt too small for me and I started picking at the geometric embroidery that encircled my waist. My mother captured my attention again by pushing one side of her hymn book into my white-gloved hands. She held her own side of the book at hip level so that I could read the music and text. She ran her velvety, white finger under the words as she sang so that I could follow them and I noticed a barely perceptible line of grey in the curved seam of her glove at the top of her index finger. Sometimes I followed the words but more often I followed the black notes dancing across the crisp, translucent vellum, rising and falling with my

17

mother's voice in a sensual, new language. Before I was old enough to go to school, my mother was teaching me through our Sunday morning hymn singing to read both words and music.

My mother's voice was lovely and sometimes people in the pew behind, I noticed, would stop singing so that they could listen to her. When I turned around to look, they started singing again. My mother would have been embarrassed if she knew. Sometimes she and I sang harmonies, but if I sang too loudly, my mother would look at me with her right eyebrow slightly raised. (She could raise her right eyebrow without raising the other. That expression was the eternal question of my childhood.) We were the pastor's wife and daughter and we could not draw attention to ourselves. We had to be dignified without being haughty and gracious without being overly friendly, my mother taught me. We were always to be polite to people and listen patiently and reply only with what was correct, not necessarily what we were thinking. We couldn't fidget while the old ladies described their most recent operations and we put on sad faces when the latest one to become a widow spoke of her grief. We never listened to the gossips and we never laughed at the ladies who were slightly crazy. Instead we smiled nicely and nodded and said, "Is that so?"

I learned all this after the services, when my mother and I would stand with my father at the church door as he greeted the parishioners. Old ladies would fuss over me and my brothers, lowering their heads to our level so that their flowered hats were in our faces. My mother would stand gracefully and with dignity beside my father. She was part of the scene and yet distant, never sharing anything of her own life, always responding sympathetically to those who shared their worries with her. She was warm and empathetic and people loved her, wanted to please her. No one ever knew how lonely she was.

I secretly believed that my mother was a queen. And my father, of course, was God.

On Sunday mornings he wore his straight, ankle-length black hassock, covered by a knee-length white alb and around his neck he wore stoles of different jewel colours as bright as fruit jellies, a different one each season of the church year. When he brought them back from the dry cleaners and hung them on the back of the kitchen door, I wanted to play dress-ups with those heavy, satin slices of emerald, amethyst, ruby and pearl, each embroidered in gold thread. I wanted to imagine what it would be like to preach to people, just as when I found my father's neatly pressed green army uniforms in the basement, I wanted to imagine what it must have been to be like him, aged seventeen, marching off to war. My father became other men in his clothes.

Sometimes I would sneak a look at him dressing in his liturgical finery before the church service. He would slick his hair back with gel from a tube and if my brothers were there, he would touch up their hair too. My father's scent was, like my mother's, spicy, except cold. Every Sunday while he was getting ready for the service, he would lift his white alb and reach through a slit in his black cassock to pull out five cents for me. I ran off to buy a coke from the red machine that rumbled and stayed lit continuously all day and all night in the church social hall.

While my father was making his transformation, my mother, my two younger brothers, Stephen and Mark, and I waited in the front pew for the service to begin. The organ always startled us with its opening blast of the processional hymn and we would start to sing, knowing that our father was beginning his procession through the sanctuary to the altar. We learned to resist the temptation to turn around and look at him. Eventually he would appear in the aisle beside us, passing through the corner of our vision, swaying from side to side, his feet steady in highly polished black brogues that were always repaired by a big, black man who never spoke and who made strong shoes you could not buy in any store. I watched my father's steady, black and white back as he walked towards the altar. He was not our father then and we were taught not to try to catch his eye. If you smiled at him, he didn't smile back. I understood that it might break the spell.

During his sermons, my father told us that we were sinners and his voice shook the altar as he told us why in great detail. When he brought his fist down on the pulpit, the trays of tiny wine glasses tinkled. Afterwards he asked us to confess our sins. The congregation buzzed and murmured: *I am heartily sorry for these my offences.* I misunderstood the line and thought that the people were "hardily" sorry. I looked for the hardiest faces, ruddy with health and sin. The service grew very dull after that, as people slowly lined up single-file to approach the altar. Women held their backs straight and men shifted their shoulders, adjusting their bodies to meet the Lord. The people kneeled at a white fence that separated my father from the congregation and they bowed their heads, eyes tightly closed, as my father fed each one the wafer and the wine and laid his hand on each head in blessing. My father's face was solemn and had a slightly concerned, immobile expression. Sometimes one of the old ladies would break the pattern of bowed heads and turn her face up gratefully towards my father's face.

"Thank you," she would whisper.

"It's alright," I read upon my father's lips. I wondered what my father had done for such ladies. I imagined him in their dark parlours, with window shades drawn, listening patiently as they wept out their troubles and gave him problems to fix.

My parents were themselves only when we got home again. "Let's kiss like eskimos," my mother would say and all three of us children would join with Mom and Dad in a circle so close that there was no air between us and we would stick out our heads and rub noses to noses, each of us making sure to rub the nose of all of the others, leaving no one out.

My parents were good and they wanted me to be. Goodness kept me in that warm circle. That was obvious from the beginning. In childhood, it was easy to be good but as I grew older it became more difficult to grasp. I wasn't allowed to date boys or wear make-up so I guarded myself and spent most of my time on reading, homework and piano. The other kids in the church called me a "goody goody", which was the greatest encouragement to be bad that there could possibly be.

"I'm normal. I'm just like you," I wanted to tell them, certain that I would have to do something very, very bad to make them believe me.

"It is hard to be different," my mother told me again and again. "But when you've grown up, you'll be glad."

When the other kids in second grade called me a nigger-lover because my best friend, Donna, was the only black girl in the class, my mother said that it was better to have one real friend with whom you could be yourself than ten friends who wanted you to conform to beliefs you considered to be wrong.

My mother had few close friends but many people loved her. She had been a pastor's daughter, too, so she was accustomed to keeping her distance from the world. She stood apart from the other women in the church. As the pastor's wife, she could not confide in them. We had to keep to ourselves as though we didn't have the same flaws as other families. Even in the late 1960s, when my mother threw away the constricting girdles and stopped wearing gloves and hats to church and, in summer, took her place in the front pew with bare, tanned legs. Even when she got a job as a teacher and went back to university to earn her Master's degree. Even when she encouraged my father to leave his post as a minister and take a job in church administration where he could use his executive skills. Even when other parents were getting divorced and remarried and there was a sexual revolution and the world was falling apart. Even then, we hid our faults from the world, like preacher's families do.

Sometimes we wondered what it would be like to not be a preacher's family and to have plenty of money like families whose fathers worked in business or in medicine. At night when I was a girl, my mother and I would drive through the rich neighbourhood and spy on the mansions, wishing we lived there. My mother drove slowly along the curb, peering through the dark into the bright rooms of the wealthy people's houses. Through undrawn draperies, we saw only fragments of rooms. The crystal fringe of a sparkling chandelier. A piece of marble fireplace. A hint of gilt mirror.

We told stories about the houses to each other. They were stage sets on which we could have played our lives. But they weren't important, not really.

When I was twelve I got a scholarship to a private school where most of the students came from wealthy families. I started to go to parties in some of those houses. One night my mother came to collect me from a particularly splendid house. I immediately started to babble to her about the band that had played and the ridiculous catered food, miniature versions of

21

meals meant for a doll's house. I asked her if caviar was really fish eggs, like the boys at the party had been saying. When I had finished, she didn't start the engine or talk. We just sat in the car in the dark for a while.

"You're in another world now. A world I'll never be a part of," she said.

I felt ashamed. I wanted to be with my mother on the outside looking in again. I wished that I had never seen the inside of those houses.

March, 1976

The numbness grew and inserted roots in that unreachable part of me. I hardly knew that it was there as I prepared to go home to my mother and my family for the spring break. I wondered if they would recognise me. I didn't. I felt at once insubstantial and grotesque. Insubstantial because I could no longer trust my own vision of myself or my perceptions of events. I had considered myself to be a musician intent about her music. The Professor had seen someone sexual and obscene. Grotesque. That meant that my reality, my version of myself, was merely an illusion. I was not the woman I thought I was: the open, ready-to-be hurt girl. I was not my mother's daughter. I was the vixen, the femme fatale. That made it hurt less, convincing myself that I had been complicitous in the event.

I didn't sleep the night before I went home. Early in the morning, I took another bath and tried again to wash off the smell and the itch of him. Then I looked at myself in the mirror. I examined the reflection of my plump, pale face in the green-tinged flourescent light. What would my mother see when she looked into my eyes? I wondered. No changes, I decided. The face in the mirror was too bland to tell its story.

An artist once told me that she could not draw my likeness because my features were too smooth. They lacked the imperfection, I realised, that creates beauty. Mine were the features of a china-headed doll: round face, pale skin, pink cheeks, pencil eyebrows and slightly slanted almond-shaped eyes, coloured unintriguingly brown.

"Bedroom eyes," a woman in my father's church once whispered to me lasciviously, pressing herself against me so that I could feel her moist breath and see the creases in her turquoise blue eyeshadow. What was her point? That I, too, was carnal beneath my plain, pastor's daughter's flesh? On the flight home I convinced myself that I could be the plain

23

daughter again. My mother would see me as I used to be. She would not see this stranger woman occupying her daughter's space. She would, by projecting her vision of my old self onto my surface, unknowingly remind me of who I had been, as easily as if she was prompting me to stand up straighter. In this way, I would gradually reclaim myself and be healed.

My father met me at the airport and I was the daughter again, but as I kept my eyes on the road and the double yellow line slithered like a snake, my fear of my homecoming grew. I could not stop myself from gathering the transparent scales of my new protective armour mile by mile.

When we arrived on our street, I was surprised to see that nothing had changed. The red-brick houses were still obstinately solid and occupied, I believed, by the unshakeable lives of the solid, waiting for me to pass through them like air.

When my father stopped the car in front of my house, I felt like I had been away for a hundred years. Looking at my mother's house was like looking at a memory and I could not remember where I fit in. We pulled into the driveway and I kept watching the house. No light flicked on. No door opened. The house seemed dead.

My father unloaded my things onto the driveway. He got back into the car and drove off to his meeting. Still, no one came running to meet me. I had to ring the bell. Silence. Then I heard someone coming to answer it, as urgently as if I had been the postman and I began to wonder, what was this homecoming?

My seventeen-year-old brother's stern face hid frightened eyes behind horned-rimmed eyeglasses.

"Hi, Kathy." He smiled a bit. He was wearing his worn, plaid flannel shirt and jeans. He looked the same and I felt guilty as soon as I saw him. I wasn't the same anymore.

"Hi, Steve."

We hugged each other. The metal screen door whipped itself closed behind me.

"Where's Mom?" I asked.

"Lying down."

"What's wrong?"

The house tasted wrong. There had been an imperceptible shift. "Mom?" I heard my voice like it was someone else's.

"Mom?" She was lying on the living room sofa.

"Hello, sweetheart," she said and smiled at me apologetically.

Something in her face had gone. My mother looked at me expectantly. I didn't know what to say. Over the previous, sleepless nights, I had thought of nothing else but how – and if – I could tell her what had happened. Now that I saw her, my daughter-self wanted desperately to confess it all. I wanted to fall into her arms in tears like a child with a cut knee. But in that moment, I knew I never would. I could not hurt her. What had happened to me was bad enough, why should she be damaged by it, too?, I thought. If she knew, the assault on her dignity would be even greater than on mine. As I looked anew at her worried face I knew that, at any cost, she must not know.

I went upstairs to my bedroom with the pale yellow wallpaper my mother had helped me to choose and the white-lace canopied bed.

I went to my bureau and opened a few of the half-empty drawers, little caskets of memories. I searched for some old, soft thing to wear, some reminder of my former self. I wanted to slip into my old self as easily as I would slip into those old clothes.

Nothing fit. This was someone else's bedroom, not mine. My fifteen-year-old brother, Mark and I cooked a dinner, under my mother's direction. My father came home and we ate. We didn't talk much. My secret overwhelmed me and made me quiet. I felt like an actress pretending that life was normal in the middle of an earthquake. I felt brittle and fake and knew I could not be my mother's daughter.

Then, after we ate, she told me.

"I'm going to the hospital tomorrow," she said. "I need you to help me take care of your brothers."

The worst was happening. She told me that a few weeks previously, she had found a lump in her breast. She was going to be admitted to hospital for the lump to be biopsied. If it was malignant, she would lose her breast. We didn't say the word.

"I'm going to be fine," she said. "There is so much they can do nowadays."

This was my fault, somehow. This was my fault.

It frightened me to see my mother loose control as she grew woozy with the pre-operative medication. Her face lost its composure and her eyes remained half-opened as her head lolled on the pillow.

"The thing I hate worst in the world is feeling out of control," she always said, explaining why she rarely took alcoholic drinks and when she did, never more than one.

The hospital was in control now. The nurses had already dressed her in a pale blue hospital gown. Her familiar cotton nightdress, soft from many washings, hung in the small hospital closet, smelling like her.

I reassured her. The lump was going to be benign. Of course it was. The chances that it would be — don't say that word — were very small. I knew that if the lump was malignant, my mother would lose her breast on the operating table. That wasn't going to happen. It would all be over tomorrow and we would still have time during my visit home to go to the museum, to a concert, have lunch and buy some clothes — a real mother and daughter's day out. We would talk and be close.

When my mother bought me clothes, I felt safe and cared for.

She hid my bulky figure beneath large sweaters and covered my legs with A-line skirts or baggy jeans.

"When I saw you getting out of the car with your parents I really felt sorry for you," one of my housemates had said when I arrived first at the conservatory. "You really should lose weight." I wore glasses and thick make-up to cover up my bad skin. My wardrobe consisted of plaid wool skirts and thick tights when most other people my age were wearing tight bluejeans and ski jackets. My best friend in high school dressed the same as me. We were comfortable, sensible and untroubled by fashion. And we were unafraid. We often joked that we looked like nuns. My clothes had let me pass directly from childhood to maturity, skipping that dangerous place in between. My mother's choices for me were my chador.

At college, I had begun to question my style, but now my clothes made sense. I was the responsible one, caring for my mother. I was mature beyond my years, my teachers always said. I wasn't swayed by frivolous, youthful temptations.

The nurses came to lay my mother on the trolley and wheel her away. I stood in the corner, watching my mother no longer being my mother but a hospital body wrapped in sheets. The nurses pushed the trolley past me and, on impulse, I bent down and kissed the rough blue cloth which lay across the breast that had fed me life. I think I must have known.

"I love you, Mom," I whispered.

Immediately, I felt embarrassed for having called attention to myself with such a theatrical, almost rude, gesture.

My mother didn't seem to notice. One of the nurses glared at me like I had done something obscene. "Come on now, we haven't much time," she snapped.

I justified my action to myself. I had been overcome by the desire to create a ritual that would embody the pain. It was a breast, an essential part of my mother, not a diseased and obsolete flap of tissue to be sliced off. "You can wait here," the nurse said. I heard my mother being wheeled away on the rattling cart. I followed the noise as long as I could, until, within seconds, it was subsumed amongst the other hospital sounds. She was gone.

As I waited for my mother to be brought back to the room, I spent the vacant hours in a daze, not knowing what to think, not knowing what not to think, praying for the best and praying that I would be able to handle the worst. These were the final, eternal, anxious hours that the accused must endure while the jury is out. It was the nervous langour that settles in when there is nothing to do because the world is about to come to an end.

I read magazines. I went for a walk in the corridor.

"Hey, you've lost weight," a man's voice called out. I turned around. It was our family doctor. His ruddy face grinned at me. How could he smile? He scarcely paused. "How'd you manage to lose that weight? Congratulations. Enjoying school?"

I didn't like him looking at my body. What did it matter if I had lost weight? How could I explain that I hadn't eaten for a week because I couldn't hold anything down and had constant diarrhoea?

"School's great," I said, being the actress again.

27

"What was that you were studying?" he asked, already moving away from down the corridor.

"Music," I said, giving him the answer he wanted, which I don't think he heard. But I wanted to say, "is my mother going to die, doctor? Please tell me the truth."

He strode off down the bright corridor without mentioning her, as though he and I were casual acquaintances who had met by chance on the street, not outside my mother's hospital room.

A few hours later, my mother returned with tubes and gauze where her breast had been. If someone had told me then, that in ten years' time, I would again be living through those anxious hours before the world ends and seeing my husband returned to me with tubes and gauze and what seemed like a death sentence where our future should be, I think I would have found a way to die.

My mother seemed to react well to the loss of her breast.

"As long as the cancer is gone, that's what's important," she kept saying. She told me stories of women she knew who had lost breasts and were living on as though nothing had happened.

"What's a breast, anyway," mother said, "just a piece of fat."

We spent timeless days in hospital waiting for test results. At first, we had been living on edge in anticipation of the discovery that either the lump was malignant or it was not.

Now we were at the second stage of praying, waiting, waiting for the doctor to tell us whether or not the cancer had spread beyond the breast.

"I'm going to be fine," my mother kept saying, smiling at me.

"Even if it has spread, I can have treatment."

She was optimistic and positive, so I copied her strength and continued to mask my dread. During the days I sat with her. In the evenings, my father visited her while I remained at home, cooking meals for my brothers and trying, although it was impossible, to take my mother's place.

I was with her when the doctor came to tell her about the test results. He told me to leave so I paced the hallway as I had seen people do in hospital dramas on television. Was this real? Or could I be dreaming? There was news being given in that room that would change our lives. When I was allowed back into my mother's room, I saw her weeping in devastation and her face, bright and optimistic moments earlier, had collapsed with grief. The cancer had spread to one of her lymph nodes. She would require chemotherapy. If it hadn't spread to the lymph nodes, she told me, she would have been okay. Now her chances were much less, she said, but she didn't speak of numbers. Fifty per cent? Thirty per cent?

I didn't ask. I tried to comfort her while she cried and she tried not to cry in order to comfort me. She was only forty-eight. There was no security in the world after that. Even though my mother insisted that she would live for many years. I wanted her to live. I needed her. So I believed that she would be alright.

We convinced ourselves that she would live indefinitely and we would remain convinced for years.

There would never be a cure. We knew that. There would be experimental chemotherapy and then the routine check-ups. Cancer would constantly remind my mother of its presence.

But my mother would have a long life, she told me, not as long a life as she could have had, but long enough. She used the word that doctors use instead of life: remission. In remission she could live for fifteen, twenty years. I would learn that living with cancer is like living with a despot who lulls you into feeling secure with his seeming benevolence, then sharply breaks the spell by leaning over your shoulder from behind, whispering, "I will take it all away from you. I will take your mother. I will take your husband, as soon as the mood stirs me to do it."

As the months passed, I grew accustomed to trimming my hopes and my mother must have too, seeking, like me, a compromise with life that would allow us to live with its shadows. She would hide as much as she could from me. I would hide as much as I could from her. We would try to protect each other.

That was the worst thing, not being able to talk to each other. I had to keep my secret from her. Her job was to get well, continue teaching and be our mother. My job was to do well in school and make her proud of me. I would forget about the past.

Back at the conservatory, my hands were jelly on the keyboard. I couldn't control them anymore. The practice room became a cell in which I would imprison myself for hours, trying to regain my musical powers, but all I heard was dull and discordant. The piano seemed permanently out of tune. I missed my first lesson with the Professor, then my second and my third. I didn't do this purposely. I simply failed to remember the time and the place. This became a habit with some of my other classes too. When I tried to read, the words didn't make sense. When I attended lectures, the teachers' words seemed utterly irrelevant. Life went on and I was only pretending to live it. Once I had been enthusiastic and lively, "a born leader" my mother used to say. I had excelled in school and she also said to me, again and again, "you have so many talents, you can be whatever you want to be." Suddenly, I didn't want be anything. I had forgotten my ambitions and desires. It was as though my body was continuing to play the role of student, sometimes turning up where it was supposed to be and sometimes not, while my mind went about other, more important business.

I was preoccupied with holding up the hope: that is what cancer forces you to do. If you stop believing in the light, it will go out, so you force yourself to keep believing. Otherwise, death will force its way in like in the dream where you hear the intruder breaking into the house and so you run downstairs and pile furniture against the door. He keeps pushing, so you push, too, with all your might so that he cannot come in. Then you live like that for years, devoting part of your energies to holding out death, part of your energies to holding up the hope, so that there is very little energy left for the everyday tasks of living. At least, that is what is was like for me.

Before I missed the fourth lesson, events took over which gave me a rest from the charade. One morning I awoke in hospital, attached to a drip, too sick to even hold down water. I wouldn't let the nurses telephone my parents because my mother was still recuperating but, eventually, the nurses convinced me that it would be necessary. A minister came to see me, at my parent's request.

"Just a tummy bug, is it?" he asked.

30

I asked myself if his face was kind and if it masked an understanding heart. Maybe this was someone to whom I could tell everything. He sat on the chair beside the bed, his eager face seeing nothing in me except one of life's minor problems. I knew then that I couldn't tell him anything at all.

"Yea, must have been something I ate," I said, smiling. I could hide a lot with my smile. I had an innocent face.

"Tell my parents I'm fine."

I was grateful to be in hospital. My hospital roommate was an assertive patient and before long she had convinced the nurses to supply us with a television set and a ration of jello and 7-up. They were ten happy days, being mothered by the nurses and given permission to be sick.

Then he broke the spell.

A nurse announced him. "Your Professor rang. He was worried about you."

My heart started to pound. "Who rang? Which Professor?"
"I'm sorry, I don't remember. He just said to tell you he's looking forward to seeing you when you're well."

He was keeping tabs on me. Back at the conservatory, I hid out in the library, in a local diner, in the students' union and, finally, persuaded myself back into my practice room. I was afraid to go there because to reach it I had to pass by the faculty room where he often sat.

My playing had deteriorated even more than before. I was supposed to play my first-year exams before the entire piano faculty at the end of the semester and I was falling apart. Determined to recover, I decided that I would practice on my own without taking lessons. I told myself that the faculty jury would be amazed at my abilities.

I threw myself into practising with renewed energy for a few days until, one evening, I looked up from the piano and saw him staring at me through the window in the practice room door. Before I could catch my breath, he was gone.

I would never be able to overcome the power of these people, I realised. There was only one way out of the Professor's studio and that was to tell the Dean of the conservatory what had happened. I couldn't do that. They would throw me out.

So keeping my secret, I stopped playing the piano and

finished the term like a sleep-walker. Near the end, the Professor approached me and told me his plan. He had rented an apartment in which I would spend the summer and he would give me daily lessons. It would transform my playing, he said. He would make me who I wanted to be.

"No. I have to go home." I thought my voice sounded muffled or maybe I was just going deaf.

"I cannot teach you to play passionately unless we have a great passion together," he actually said.

I walked away from him. It wasn't amusing then.

"What is it you do to me?" he called after me.

There were no words to describe what I had done to him. I understood finally, or so I thought, what had happened. He wanted me to be his mistress. Obviously, I had unconsciously conveyed the impression that I was available. And with this thought, my secret began to gain new meanings. I was no longer just the victim, but the perpetrator, too.

Of course I couldn't tell her.

I never played the piano again. It wasn't a conscious decision. It just evolved that way. There was no joy in playing and so there was no point.

I returned home for the summer. My mother and I moved uneasily together as though we didn't fit our skins. My secret had grown so enormous that I couldn't speak without divulging it and so we didn't speak. My mother tried to communicate with me but I spurned her motherly advances. If she touched one crack, I would break. I decided that I would cope on my own and not burden her with my problems, so it was in a matter-of-fact way that I told her I wasn't returning to the conservatory.

"Why?"

"I don't like it. It's boring."

"But you love music."

There was no career to be made out of playing classical music, I told her. I would probably end up as a music teacher, a dull prospect. She didn't believe me.

"What happened?" she asked.

Without thinking, I began to throw off my armour and plunged ahead.

"He was interested in me, Mom."

32

"What do you mean?"

"He didn't see me as just a student." I felt I had to protect her by speaking in code.

"Was he interested in you — romantically?"

The tension in her voice warned me to proceed with care.

"Yea."

"Did he touch you?"

"I guess so."

"How did he touch you?"

I didn't want her to think badly of me.

"Like a man touches you, I guess."

I meant this as a preliminary piece of information but I could not tell her anymore. I had already told her enough to destroy her faith in me.

"What did you say to him?" she demanded.

She was enraged at him already and I could hear her voice starting to shatter. Be my mother, I kept thinking. Don't change. Please see me as you always did.

"What did he do to you?"

"He tried to kiss me, that's all."

"I'm going to call the conservatory."

"Mom, don't."

"It's wrong."

"I know, but don't call them."

A few days later, she told me what had happened. She had phoned the Dean of the conservatory and told him in her calm, polite way how angry she was that a teacher could try to become sexually involved with a student.

The Dean had been condescending and dismissive. "You must understand that these things happen, Mrs Holmquist."

When she repeated for me what he had said, her voice was clouded with angry tears.

I hated the Dean for refusing to believe that the Professor's actions were unwanted.

I hated him more for insulting my mother.

She was not naive but neither did she live in a world where "these things" happened. I knew the Dean's words were an assault on her dignity. And mine: he saw me as a thing that had happened and probably as a thing waiting to happen again. It confirmed what I already knew, that no matter how

33

painful or humiliating, it hadn't been serious and that, at least partly, it had been my fault. His words implied that the incident had been a two-way business. His words also placed between my mother and myself a fragment of doubt that couldn't be explained unless I told her the whole story, which I was not prepared to do. I had to protect her from the whole truth and thereby protect myself from the full harm of the event. Her knowing the details of what he had done would be worse than the thing itself.

If I could not be myself anymore, at least I could remain myself in her eyes.

We stopped talking about it after that. We knew enough about each other.

"You've grown hard," she would say to me months later.

I suppose that is what the cancer did to me. It finished what the Professor started and forced me to become hard. Otherwise I would have fallen apart. The hard shell held in a chaotic mess of emotions. I didn't understand myself then, however, and only felt guilty — and a little proud — for being hard. Although, looking back, I disagree with my mother. I wasn't hard; I was apathetic. I still couldn't explain to her what had happened to me. I couldn't tell her that the world had come to an end that day in the Professor's studio and that I was merely a ghost passing through the wreckage, looking for its bones.

October 1976

So my mother never knew the details of the crucial event that spun us apart and how it made me feel, just as I never knew precisely what the doctors told her. She only observed the after-effects in me, found bits of debris scattered here and there and tried to trace them to their source. What she discovered about me terrified her.

She reeled when she found the package of contraceptive pills on top of my bureau. I had left the conservatory behind me like a bad dream. I was again the daughter she wanted me to be, studying theatre and English literature at an elite college and having what one might call a normal life. I was no different than my college friends. "The pill" was handed out freely to us by the college clinic. But I was different from my mother. While I'm sure she did not expect me to remain a virgin until I married like she had, she had wanted me to wait a while, until I found someone who loved me.

After my mother died, Mark found a black-and-white photograph of my mother at the age of about twenty-one, which captured her perfectly. The photograph was taken from a balcony looking down onto a ballroom floor. Whoever took the photograph must have been enraptured by my mother's tendency to stand off by herself musing and looking completely self-contained as though the world was of little consequence to her. My mother stands in the centre of the photograph in the middle of the vast, polished floor, alone.

Somehow above it all, she is looking off into the distance in that dreamy way of hers. She is wearing a taffeta and chiffon ballgown which, I think, must have been coloured champagne. The dress has a long, full skirt and a nipped-in waist. Its shapely, draped bodice has a high schoolmarm collar. It sets off her neat figure and high bustline prudishly and yet not. A gaggle of girls stand gossiping to one side. They're looking over their shoulders, caught up in the chase. A few young men stand in the distance behind my mother, watching her. They set my mother off like courtiers around a queen. If I had a time machine, I would ask to visit that dance so that I could watch my mother.

When I was a little girl, she told me many times about her social life at college. She refused to join a sorority and started her own group of independent women, impressing the sorority women so much that she ended up president of the women students' organisation. My ideas about dating were infused with my mother's stories. I thought that I could not fall in love until I had been to that dance. I believed that I could not be made love to until I had danced with that line of courteous young men who wanted me to marry them.

When I saw the photograph 10 years after my mother's death, I was startled to see hard evidence which proved that my childhood image of my mother had actually been real. And I was reminded that something of myself had been lost when I had been unable to fulfill that romantic image. But there was no going back. The world wasn't like that anymore. That's what I told my mother the day she found the pills.

When she found them, she didn't tell me right away. Then a few hours or days later, I don't remember, she took me shopping. Our major mother-daughter conversations were always conducted while out shopping, in that woman-space between the lingerie department and the lunch counter. This time, she didn't even wait until we got to the shopping centre. From the driver's seat, she asked, "why do you need contraception?"

"Why do you think?" I said, laughing like it was nothing.

"I didn't think you were ready for that."

I was ready, I thought. Explaining myself to my mother, I looked straight ahead at the road and spouted common-sense (I believed), telling her that everyone at college had relationships and nobody wanted to get pregnant and so everyone was responsible and on the pill. My mother, who had never done what "everyone" did and encouraged me to be just as independent, tried to explain that sex was part of a loving relationship. I didn't let her finish and shut her up with my seemingly self-confident talk about the way things were now, compared to when she was young.

I must have sounded naive and as analytical as a radio talk show sex therapist. My mother's eyes turned red with tears. It didn't occur to me, then, to ask myself why she was crying. I assumed she was angry at me because I had rejected her strict sense of morality. She always cried when she was angry, never shouted. Thirteen years later, and she gone for eleven of them, I finally understand why she was crying.

I didn't talk about being loved or loving. And although I may have thought I was involved in a relationship, there was no evidence in my life that anyone cared for me deeply. When I was a little girl, my mother told me that sex was something that a man and a woman did when they loved each other so much that they wanted to become one person. There was no one I wanted to become one person with, or who wanted to become one person with me. I was alone and fighting for my life. I was just as alone with my boyfriend as I was away from him.

I think she must have known.

When I talked to her dishonestly, because I couldn't even be honest with myself, she knew I was discordant. She knew that I wanted to be loved more than anything in the world and that I kept choosing the wrong men, who exploited my desire. My mother, in her dying world, could do nothing to help me. She could only watch the progress of my yearning and wish, I see now, that she could stop my pain. She cried because she was unable to stop me from continuing my painful journey. The road was embedded too deeply inside me.

"My father was never affectionate with me," she told me once, and added, "My parents weren't the hugging type." I think that is where she believed the road began.

"I was like you," she told me another time, "I always fell in love with older men, especially my male teachers."

But she had done nothing as terrible as I had done as I tried to erase my memories. The young men that truly cared about me frightened me. I chose others, who never lasted. The more I fell in love, the worse it got and the worse they treated me the more I felt I deserved it but I didn't enjoy it and I couldn't explain it. I wanted what they couldn't give me: to be erased and replaced by their image of me; to be made real by a place in someone else's life.

My mother only saw pieces of this picture. I lived a secret life, while pretending to be the good daughter, until the falseness became to much to bear.

I left school at the end of my third year and ran away to Paris with Clive who promised things he couldn't deliver.

I told her I was going to Paris to work in the theatre, which was true, but I didn't tell her the whole story. I didn't know it then, but my mother had only two years left to live. I spent her penultimate year away from her, separated by more than the Atlantic, feeling too guilty to call, too guilty to write, too guilty to fall asleep without wine and believing that by escaping I was saving my sanity. I believed that I had found the mission that would give me a purpose, a cult of two.

My father wrote me a letter telling me that I should come home because my mother was very sick. Then she wrote to say this wasn't true. When I spoke to her on the phone that Christmas, she wept so much that she couldn't speak to me. When I asked her about her health, she insisted that she was well. Shortly after she died, eighteen months after that phone call, my father told me that she had cried every night that I was in Paris. Then, seven years after she died, her friend, Barb, told me: "Your mother was so happy that you were able to live in Europe that year. She thought it was a great experience for you."

I am sure that both these statements were true. By secretly guarding her grief, she allowed me to escape. Even later, when she knew more about my relationship with Clive, she left me to make my own decisions despite the fact that she detested him. She knew why I was with him and maybe she also knew that neither she nor I was strong enough to release me from his grasp.

Yes, she knew where the road started. A decade after she was dead, her brother and sister, my Uncle Alan and Aunt Ruth, whose faces were so like my mother's that I had only recently lost my fear of looking at them, brought me and my husband back to the house where my mother was born on King Street in Pontiac, Rhode Island.

Aunt Ruth drove us in the ancient car which had belonged to my Uncle Harold, my mother's eldest brother, who died suddenly only a year or two after my mother but whose car had refused to die. Harold's Korean wife, Su, believed that the car embodied something of Harold's spirit. Su and Harold had lived in Washington, D.C., five hundred miles from where Harold was buried in the family plot beside St Paul's Lutheran Church in Pontiac, so Su had entrusted Aunt Ruth with the duty of keeping my Uncle Harold's car and driving it occasionally to his graveside. So as we approached Pontiac, the scene of my mother's childhood, it was like being transported into the past by the spirits of the dead, not by a car at all.

When we reached Pontiac, my Aunt Ruth and Uncle Alan, as deftly as archaeologists, began to gently uncover the origins of the town, making me see past the shopping malls and industrial parks and highways and tracts of new houses that had obliterated the country landscape they had grown up in. They had stories to tell about each building that we passed. We paused before the pile of nineteenth century bricks that had once been the madhouse, where my teenaged mother had worked to earn money for college and where, on full-mooned nights, she told me, the inmates howled like animals. We passed the closed-down mill where my Uncle Alan had worked for many years, supplying my mother with flower-sprigged fabric that she used to make my dresses.

We passed the river where my uncles had fished and swam and wiled away their childhood summers before the war. We passed the houses of people who were dead, whose children were dead, but who came instantly alive as my Uncle Alan, beside me in the back seat, told us their histories. He made us laugh with his thumbnail sketches of these people who were under the ground and who, by our laughter, were temporarily raised from the dead. He resurrected my own childhood, too, for these were the same stories that he told me, my brothers and cousins when we were children, keeping us up late with laughter, during those magical summer reunions on Cape Cod when we would all play together at the beach. The children of Pontiac who he brought back to life were always bolder and more wicked than real children and their sole reason for living seemed to be the humiliation of adults. And in the telling, my Uncle Alan brought back to life my mother. These were the stories that had made my mother laugh so hard that she cried and whimpered, "stop, Alan." When my Aunt Ruth

39

laughed from behind the wheel, I could hear the undertone of my mother laughing with her.

Skimming along through Pontiac in a car fueled by stories and powered by a ghost, we finally reached the house. Forty years previously, when my mother and her five brothers and sisters, Aunt Ruth, Uncle Alan, Uncle Harold, Uncle Pete and Aunt Helen, were children, it had been the pastor's house, underpinning the small country town.

In the decades which followed the death of my grandparents, the Swedish pastor and his wife, King Street had gradually become a forgotten corner of an anonymous suburb. The large, portly house had lost its context and so, much of its presence. Once immaculately kept, it had become a tumble of rented rooms. Like markers for time-travellers, the shade trees my grandfather planted were still there, although there was no trace of my grandmother's elaborate garden, a glimpse of which I had seen in the background of photographs in which my mother stood with her three solemn-faced young brothers in their army uniforms and her two graceful sisters, all of them eternally young, tall and strong.

The car idled quietly as we sat for a moment with our memories on King Street. I leaned my head out of the car window and looked past the present and through the gable window into the former life of the house, at my teenaged mother lying in her bed on an early winter morning, shivering under the covers and waiting for the last possible moment to get up and get dressed. On Sunday mornings, she had told me, she often risked her father's wrath by savouring those last moments in bed. She waited until she heard him setting off for the white, spindle-spired St Paul's on the hill. Then she jumped out of bed and from her window, I imagined, she saw her father dressed in his black frock preacher's coat and starched linen bib, beginning his stern procession through the sedate streets of the town.

Shivering in pure white bloomers and slip, my mother rushed to dress. Moments later, the preacher's daughter emerged from the house, wearing her plain, dark blue jacket and skirt, her dark brown overcoat and brown velvet hat, kid leather gloves and on her feet, burnished brown high-heeled, sling-backs.

I thought again of my mother as she appeared in that photograph, dressed for the ball.

"Your mother was so popular," Aunt Ruth told me from the front seat of the car. "Your grandfather couldn't understand it. He assumed that to have so many boys wanting to marry her she must have done something."

Aunt Ruth gave me a yellowed newspaper clipping which showed a photograph of my beautiful 18-year-old mother in her vintage 1940s going-away-to-college suit, ringing the church bell. "The Belle of Pontiac," the caption read. I thought of the guilt my mother must have felt for doing nothing. I wanted to go back in time and rearrange events. I wanted to stop my mother from becoming disappointed in her life and to prevent the sorrows that beat her down. And I wanted to speak to her and redeem myself in her clear, eighteen-year-old eyes.

My mind skipped on to the scene that must have occurred after church, when the family sat down to dinner. Through the dining room window, I saw my stern grandfather, the pastor who with little more than his Latin, Greek and philosophy had emigrated to the United States from Sweden as a young man and who now presided at the head of the table, maintaining strict control over his six strong children like a sailor trimming the sheets, simultaneously predicting and defying their emotions. He must have set the sails of my mother like a Viking coffin ship, the course headed straight to sea with ropes tied in inscrutable knots that gave my mother no choice but to take the inevitable course and capsize under the strength of the wind in deep waters, because her sails could not change with the wind.

My grandfather would have seen only one course. He would have told his children that they abided with him in the temple or they were flung out. As they listened, their heads bowed in shame, a warm breeze rippled the lace curtains at the window, fluttering with a future tense that, decades later, would see me cast out. In the future, when she was angry with her daughter, my mother would express her disapproval through silences, never through anger: silences which meant the withdrawal of love.

For a long time I thought that because my mother was

brought up by her father to be morally rigid, she had no idea what I was going through. Looking back after she was gone, I realised that she knew my story more comprehensively than I did myself. She had been the daughter hungry to be loved. She had seen my reasons yet she had not tried to stop me. She had both respected and feared my need to take my own path. I finally understood her, sitting outside the house on King Street, but it was too late to tell her that I did. "Talk to her. Soon it will be too late," I told myself over and over again as she lay dying.

The misunderstanding, or perhaps, the fear of misunderstanding, that lay between us was so great that when I watched my mother being eaten away by cancer, I feared that she was dying young, a mere twenty-three years after my birth, so that I could live. My great secret was that I was anticipating the release which would be brought by her death. I would not have to hide my true self from her anymore, fearing her disapproval. I did not want to lose her, but I could not bear to fail her. Again and again, I had made choices which caused her pain.

I am sorry, Mother. So many times I have wanted to tell you: I am sorry. I did not want to make you cry.

There was no release with her death. The pain continued as it had gone before. I felt I had no right to enjoy my life while she was dying, even though she insisted that she was going to live. And when she finally passed away, I had no right to exist in her absence. Until, outside that house on King Street, when for a moment I felt the original life of my mother's early years continuing beneath the shallow surface of the present, I realised that I, like the new highways and shopping malls, had been built upon layers of previous lives whose sorrows and regrets kept rising to the surface, creating the concoction of generations that had patterned my life and determined its course.

Summer 1979 - Spring 1980

My mother wept when I called her from London that June to tell her that I was coming home. I had decided to finish my final year of college.

"That's wonderful," she said. "When?"

"August first," I told her.

"August?" she asked, suddenly subdued.

I announced that I planned to spend six weeks in Ireland first. I wanted to make the most of my time left in Europe. August would be time enough.

"August is so far away," she said. August is far away when you have been told you may not live that long. But it didn't seem far away to me. I didn't know that my mother was counting days preciously. I was so bent on my own destiny that I didn't think of her's. I had received no warnings about my mother's health since the previous Christmas and I believed all she said in her letters. All was well. I believed that she would always be there for me to come home to. Even when I was far away from her, I felt that I was with her. She was constant and eternal. That June, there was a place and an adventure that I preferred over her. Clive may not always be there, I thought.

I saw my homecoming for the month of August almost as an obligatory gesture before starting college again in September. My duty was to finish my senior year of college for my mother. I owed it to her. I didn't know then that I owed it to myself.

"Okay, August," she said, resigned to my attempts to convince her this was best for me. "If you change your mind, just phone us, okay? We'll send you the ticket."

"Okay, Mom. I love you."

"I love you, too. We can't wait to see you," she said.

I felt sick hearing the sadness in her voice. The sickness lasted. I was staying in a house in Pimlico. It was hot. Diesel trains ran along a track at the back of the house all night long. I sweated to their roar and couldn't sleep for three nights. I loved her so much. I didn't want to stay away and yet I couldn't go home to her because some unmet need was driving me to spend that cold, Irish summer with Clive unpleasantly in limbo and unhappily caught between one kind of parent and another.

In August, I flew home to the family's beach house in Chatham, Massachusetts.

"I've never seen you so thin," my mother said.

At first, there was silence. Then I tried to explain myself in between the silences and tried to pretend that nothing had changed. I could be the plain daughter again.

Then, about two weeks after I arrived home, my father tried to tell me once more that my mother was dying. We were driving to the town clinic because I needed a physical examination before being readmitted to college. I can still remember the exact place where we were on Main Street.

"They opened her up," my father told me. "The surgeon said that when he ran his hand over her liver, he could feel the cancer on its surface, like grains of sand."

Seconds later, we pulled into the parking lot in front of the clinic. Dizzy, I sat in the waiting room, feeling afraid. When the doctor examined me, he said, "your blood pressure is very high for someone your age."

I didn't tell him why.

I walked slowly outside to the car where my father was waiting and we drove back to the house. It was mid-afternoon. Everyone else was at the beach. The house ticked away to itself. It seemed brittle as a shell. I put on my bathing suit and went down to the beach, to my mother's beach where we had spent two decades worth of summers. It was the beach where we had experienced real joy and it was my mother's favourite place in the world.

I saw her in the distance, lying on the sand with her head leaning back and her face tilted towards the sun. She had covered her head with her floppy, wide-brimmed yellow hat to protect her skin that glowed with sun and oil. Even then, she was preserving herself as though she had decades left to live. She looked stylish in her black bathing suit and her big

Jackie O sunglasses and as I got closer, I could see her brown legs stretching towards the water. Then I noticed that her hair was damp. She must have just finished swimming in that graceful way of hers.

Your long, slow side-stroke, water dancer.

As I moved closer, I saw her wriggling toes covered in thousands of grains of hot, yellow sand. No, she wouldn't die: she would not, I told myself. If we didn't talk about it, it wouldn't happen.

When my mother said that she was going to be fine, I would believe her. I would let her push me away.

Once, I asked.

"Mom. Dad says you're really sick."

"Your father is exaggerating," she said. I returned to college and applied myself to my studies as I had in high school before my experience at the conservatory. I wanted to do well for my mother's sake and being away for a year had given me a greater sense of myself and put college in perspective.

Ever since the incident with the Professor, I had felt conned by those in power. I felt like a victim who could never fit in. After the year away in Europe, I still felt that I would never belong in that hypocritical academic system where female students were considered to be fair game. I would never succeed on their terms, I believed. But at least I had a stronger sense of my own intelligence and I was able to do well.

I spoke to my mother almost nightly on the telephone. She looked forward to my call and always sounded delighted as though she hadn't heard from me in months. One of the things we talked about was my experience with the Professor but I remained guarded and spoke to her about it in terms of sexual harassment. She encouraged me to find people in the college who were sympathetic and to try to raise awareness so that it wouldn't happen again to another student.

She also spoke to my brothers nearly every night. Both were away at college. Mark, the youngest, had just started his freshman year so that my mother was without a child in her house for the first time since I was born. My father had new responsibilities in his job which occasionally took him away on business. During the day, my mother continued to teach. But the long evenings must have been hard on her.

I didn't realise then how lonely she was. Only afterwards did she tell me. I put myself in her place. I imagined her coming home from school, burdened with books and papers and a shopping bag full of groceries. I saw her fumbling for her keys in the winter dark then opening the door on an empty house. I never knew her to be alone. I only knew her when the house was full of the noise and activity created by my brothers and me. She must have longed for us even as she was pushing us away. What did she have to look forward to, except dying?

During those long evenings shared long-distance, we chronicled our lives for her and when the phone bills came, she paid them without complaining. At the time, I didn't ask why.

"When I do die, it will be from the cancer, but I will live a long time first," she said.

And then it was Christmas, John Lennon was murdered and I was going home. It was our last Christmas together before my mother died but I didn't know that then. Each time my father tried to tell me that she was dying, my mother denied it and insisted that life would continue as it always had. I preferred to accept her reality. Many months later, I would finally hear from her doctor that she was dying and the news would be as shocking to me as if my mother had been shot on the street by a deranged killer.

Mom was going to live a long time first. That is what I believed that last Christmas.

But as I drank in the sense of home, I still had an undertaste of knowledge that home would soon die with my mother. This awareness hung over us like a net waiting to drop and trap us. We were paralysed with sadness, unable to accept the reason for our sadness and not talking about it either.

Each of us in the family feared what was happening and each of us suffered silently.

My brothers and I kept faithfully to our family traditions as though we were still children untainted by the world. We shopped for presents on Christmas Eve and decorated the tree with the same bright objects we had used for twenty years. We immersed ourselves in preparations as though by making the external details right, we could make the centre hold.

As I watched my mother prepare the food for our Swedish

46

Christmas Eve dinner, I tried to memorise each detail of her movements so that I would be able to reproduce the meal later as her stand-in. My father put it into my head.

"You should learn from your mother how to make her pastry. No one makes pastry like your mother," he said. His real message was *learn now, before it is too late*.

It had never occured to me before to ask my mother to pass on her ability to make pastry. It was unique to her cool fingers, so delicate compared to mine. (Even now, I can only fit her wedding ring on my little finger.) She always used a big yellow bowl and filled it with silken flour then made a hollow in the centre where she placed the shortening.

She flaked the flour and fat together with quick, light, fingertips, then added ice water to make the pastry congeal. No more than absolutely necessary. That was the secret.

Throughout that day with the distance of an anthropologist I continued my unconscious cataloguing of my mother. I watched her take the black iron pestle and mortar that had been her mother's from its high shelf above the stove. She used it to pulverise cardamom seeds for the Swedish coffee bread. I observed the way she kneaded the eggy, yeasty, fragrant dough until it was pliable and shiny. The ball of golden dough was so full of yeast that it seemed alive. It was smooth as skin on the surface and spongy to the touch. My mother placed the dough in the bottom of the deep yellow bowl where it looked small and then she covered it with a clean tea-towel. We waited for it to swell to many times its size. When it filled the bowl like a pregnant belly and seemed to be about to burst over the rim, my mother lifted the towel. She made a fist and with one swift punch deflated the fragrant mound which gasped in surprise. The dough continued to whoosh softly as it yielded its air to my mother's kneading hands. Then she left it to silently rise again as she got started on the Swedish meatballs. When she pinched the nutmeg from its jar, I watched. When she grew tired and rubbed her forehead with the back of her hands, greasy from rolling meatballs, I watched.

"Brown them quickly," she said, "then leave them to steam in their own juices." It was an art so deft that she didn't trust me to do it myself.

Then she showed me the Swedish tradition of stirring a single, pale almond into the rice pudding before it was baked.

"Whoever finds it will be lucky for the rest of the year," she said. I wanted her to find it. And I thought about her childhood Christmases, when she and her brothers and sisters got presents of oranges and nuts and were grateful. They were satisfied with one present each, unlike us who received several presents each, so many that there wasn't enough room under the tree. My mother spoiled us with gifts that Christmas more than any other.

I helped her time the pudding in the oven.

"You take it out when the centre is still slightly soft," she said. Then she plunged a clean, silver knife not into the heart of the dish, but between the centre and the rim.

"If the knife comes out clean, it's done," she said.

She and I colluded in this passing on of tradition, still unable to admit to each other why were doing it. We went through the motions and pretended to be a normal mother and daughter on Christmas Eve like hypnotised dancers, swaying to music that only we could hear.

When I was a small child, cooking with my mother was one of my favourite pastimes. She and I had our own routine. The local Baltimore television channel had a cooking programme and I used to love to watch the programme's hostess preparing her dishes. She always had the precisely correct amounts of ingredients ready to use in little glass dishes: a quarter cup of butter, a cup of sugar, a teaspoon of cinnamon. I loved to measure, so my mother and I used to pretend that we had our own cooking programme. My mother would be the cook and I would be her assistant.

"And now my lovely assistant, Kathryn, will pour two cups of flour into the bowl," my mother would say. And I would pose with the flour as though I was one of those pretty models on television game shows displaying a refrigerator.

"Mmm, flour, it's good," I said to the imaginary television camera behind the sugar canister.

Cooking with my mother that last Christmas I felt like a charlatan. We were no longer that close, even though we wanted to be. Once we were a unit so tight that I had been terrified to part from her. Leaving home for the conservatory

48

four years previously, I had feared that when I left, our world would fall apart. And when that happened, we couldn't tell each other why. Maybe we were too frightened of what we would discover about each other. Maybe it was just that we had lost the intimacy of mother and child and not yet mastered the intimacy of women. Maybe we hid our pain too well.

Last thing that Christmas Eve night, my mother returned to the dough, puffy again and even plumper than before. This time she asked me to punch it down and I felt the dough collapse around my fist. She showed me how to shape it into long braids. Then we left it to rise again overnight, ready for baking early Christmas morning.

Only now, as I write this, have I thought what it must have been like for my mother to awaken early Christmas morning to put her bread in the oven, knowing deep inside herself that this was the last time.

We survived Christmas Day, each of us trying our best to make it memorable. Underneath the formality of good intentions, that screaming thought resounded: "This could be the last time." But no one dared to speak it. During the week following Christmas, my mother was extremely tired and spent a lot of time sleeping on the couch in the living room. She seemed depressed and it was hard to make her laugh. Mark always found a way to make her face crack into laughter despite her self-control. Because he was the last one to leave home, Mark had spent more time alone with her than I had and he knew her like a friend. My brothers hadn't disappointed her like I had. They were her gallant boys and carried her dignity into the world.

I continued to disturb her through my attachment to Clive and I felt I had to mislead her about the amount of time I was spending with him. My secret made me feel like a criminal but I needed to keep him in reserve. I foolishly believed that when one anchor was pulled up I would need another.

I had two weeks' holidays from school but instead of spending the entire time with my mother, I left home a few days early to visit Clive. He was lonely, he said and made me feel so guilty that I tore myself away from my mother to be with him. With hindsight, I would wish that I had remained at home those last few days. I would not regret one day begrudged Clive whom I would grow to despise and I would beg God for just five more minutes with my mother. That final Christmas, my mother must have wanted me to stay yet she never made her wishes known. Her love let me fly.

April-June, 1980

I returned home to my mother one more time, to bring her home. Women tell me that the overwhelming demands of bringing a child into the world, both consume the mother and make her replete. My mother's dying was like that. For eight harrowing weeks, death upset the rhythm of night and day and consumed me as deftly as it trapped my mother. But where a child brings the fullness of life, death brought another sensation: a feeling of having gorged on emptiness.

I didn't know this was going to happen. I had never seriously considered the possibility that my mother would die, much less the practical matters of how she would die and who would care for her. I didn't know that in the end we would be abandoned by the doctors and that my own responsibilities as her only daughter would be overwhelming.

Her dying began for me in late April when I was completing my final semester of college and preparing to graduate. I still wasn't aware that she was terminally ill. My father had told me again that my mother was dying but she continued to deny it. I was confused and decided to go straight to the source. I telephoned her doctor in Baltimore.

"You mean you don't know?" he asked in disbelief. There was a brief silence before he sliced through my doubts.

"Your mother has a few weeks at most," he said. I heard resentment in his voice. "More than a year ago I told her she had three months," he continued. "She just will not give up. She refuses to accept it."

How does one accept death?

He was accusing her of defying his predictions. Building up his case, the doctor described how she reacted to his pronouncement of her sentence. She had not sat calmly in the chair before his desk and replied, "thank you, doctor." She had rebelled. She had shown that she was afraid. His words slipped by me, wriggled from my fingers.

"How much time does she have?" I asked.

He made a dismissive sound, "hmph."

"How long?"

"I don't know. It's like I said."

"How long will it be?" I asked again. I would fly home immediately. I knew that now. Oh God, why hadn't she told me?

"It will be weeks rather than months," he said with an air as irritated as if I had asked him to predict the weather.

My mother was a failure as far her doctor was concerned.

He would show me again before long that he resented her audacity in refusing to die gracefully.

When I hung up the phone, I wanted to run to someone. I wanted to repeat the doctor's words to someone wiser on the chance that perhaps I hadn't heard him right. Maybe his message would lose its fatal meaning under a more favourable interpretation.

Maybe there will be a miracle.

I felt that I was living in a nightmare.

Mom is going to die. It can't be true.

Ten years later, I would still be having that nightmare in which my mother was alive and healthy and then someone would tell me that she was going to die. That latent pain would always split me afresh in my dreams just as it split me after my phone call to the doctor.

Ten years later, some deep part of me would still be reluctant to accept the truth.

That day in April, 1979, standing alone in the phone booth, I needed someone to confirm that I was still living in reality. My illusions that my mother would live were reluctant to disintegrate. I felt that I had been pulled from life through the veil that screens the living from the truth. I was a new arrival in the death world and I couldn't find my bearings.

Her suffering replayed itself in my mind. For four years after being diagnosed as having cancer, my mother had clung to life and remained inspiringly positive. How could hope vanish with one phone call?

The facts of my mother's illness were still unclear to me then. I would eventually discover that, just like she said, the breast cancer never came back. She was four years clear of it

52

which meant that her chances of survival for 15 years or more were excellent. And then against almost impossible odds, a second, unrelated cancer had taken advantage of her fatigue and slowly turned her healthy cells into the malignant tumours that would kill her. During the years that my mother was overcoming one form of cancer, she unknowingly harboured a second fatal growth. At the same time I was growing away from her. Ignoring her. Sloughing her off like dead skin. All the while she had encouraged me to travel and to become independent. She had pushed me to complete my final year of college five hundred miles away from her. The last time I had seen her, during spring break, she had acted as though we would always continue the way we were, loving but slightly bored with each other and aching to make other connections. She had asked nothing of me.

"Why didn't you tell me?" I wanted to shout at her. "Why didn't you tell me that you were already supposed to be dead?"

If I had known, I would have spent the year at home caring for her. I wouldn't have let her spend all those days and nights alone in the house while my father was away on business.

She didn't even tell me that earlier that spring she had been forced to quit her teaching job. During those long phone conversations her voice had never changed.

While her body was being ravaged by cancer, she had let me imagine her still looking the same and continuing our family life in her gentle, concerned way even though her family was gone.

Why hadn't I stayed with her? Why was I so anxious to escape the anxiety of being with her, sensing she was unwell? Why did her pain make me run away? I had cared only for rescuing myself.

And there was the enormity of her secret: every time she had said goodbye she had known that it might have been the last goodbye. I should have sensed that. I should have been a better daughter.

As I ran the words of the doctor's hopeless message through my mind, I gradually realised why my mother had been hanging onto life. The doctor had made it obvious that he saw my mother as a troublesome patient who would not admit that she had taken enough suffering and instead kept hanging stubbornly on. But I knew her desire to hang onto life was not selfish. I knew she was hanging on, not only for herself, but for me and my brothers. Consciously or not, she was timing her death. She wanted my brothers to get through the academic year, then have the summer to recover from her death. She wanted to see me finish college. I was the eldest and at least if she survived long enough, she could witness that first graduation ceremony and only imagine the two which would follow.

She knew that she would die never knowing what had happened to the children she had nurtured for more than twenty years. She knew that her destiny would be to accompany us on the road as far as she was allowed to walk and then to turn and leave us, taking with her only her faith that somehow we would manage. How well I knew the manner of her death. She was conducting it as she had when we were children and afraid to go to school. She was bringing us to the door, encouraging us to go in, telling us she would stay, then quietly waiting for us to become absorbed in the activities of the other children so that when she finally left, we would not notice that she had gone. When we looked up and saw that she wasn't there, we would scarcely notice. And so with her death, she hoped, the momentum of our lives would carry us over the sorrow.

So I could not tell her that I knew. Speaking to her on the phone on the same day that I spoke to her doctor, I colluded in the conspiracy against death. I finished the semester, feeling like a diver hanging permanently in midair at the edge of a cliff, with no ground under me, but not yet knowing how I would fall and powered by a continuous surge of adrenalin, keeping me tensely suspended.

On graduation day, May fifth, death and I were formally introduced and I began my slow fall.

My initiation into becoming my mother's carer was to borrow a wheelchair from the college's student services office. I had never pushed a wheelchair before. Wheelchairs were things that other people needed, not us. I still couldn't believe that my mother was an invalid. I pushed the empty chair to meet my parents at the inn where they were staying. It was the same inn in which the three of us had stayed four years previously, the night before I first met the Professor.

I pushed the chair down the corridor past doors which all looked the same, past mundanely furnished rooms which contained sets of normal-looking parents in town for their children's graduations. My father was expecting me and poked his head out of one of the rooms to wave me in. And then I saw it commanding the centre of the anonymous hotel room. Seated on the edge of the bed, with its shoulders slumped and its neck barely able to hold up its head, was death in the body of my mother, smiling at me.

She had dressed in bright colours: fuschia and spring green. On her eyelids, she had attempted to brush some blue eyeshadow and had missed. Her mascara was pathetically smudged underneath her eyelashes.

"How do I look?" she asked me shyly.

"You look beautiful," I said, wetting my finger with my tongue so that I could wipe away the mascara smudge.

"Oh, did I mess it up?" she asked.

"No, it's fine now. See?" I said.

She avoided looking in the mirror. Her face fell in disappointment. The smudged eye make-up was another sign that she was losing her control over her body, losing life. Somehow I just knew that. I knew that this small failing was one of a string of uneventful disappointments that reminded her daily of her disintegration.

I tried not to show my fear as I looked into her almost unrecognisable face. She had aged thirty years in the three months since I had seen her last. Her beautiful face had become a skull. Her soft olive skin had turned sallow. Her curly auburn hair had thinned and lost its sheen. Her hazel eyes were glazed with that look of suffering that transfixes the faces of the dying and makes them look as though they are seeing beyond us, perceiving the world we are living in as a transparent film transposed upon the deeper, real world of eternity.

I hated that graduation day. The happiness of the other students and their parents as they proudly posed for photographs seemed absurd and unfair. The tradition at the college was to hold the commencement ceremony outdoors

55

in the town square. It lasted for hours and the sun was so hot that my mother couldn't take it. She sat in her wheelchair, holding herself erect in her dignified way while the sun made her sick. When I was given my diploma, I waved from the platform across the crowd so that she could see me.

My father took a picture of me smiling in the same way as all the other students smiled. In the picture, I was giving a little victory salute. Beneath my happy mask I was terrified and ashamed.

After receiving my diploma, I walked like the other students past a cordon of professors in their ceremonial gowns. As I did so, several of the women professors stepped out of line, one by one, and came forward to congratulate me as though I was an honour student or a valedictorian. They were thanking me through their gesture for my courage in helping to set up the college's sexual harassment committee, which is still operating to this day. It meant more to me than my diploma. It meant a lot to my mother, too.

I was embarrassed about that bit of paper. It did not contain my actual degree. I had been too upset to finish two of my final essays and one of my exams and my professors had told me not to worry, that later in the summer I could finish them at home and send them in and then I would be granted my degree. So the diploma I showed my mother was an ersatz one. She held it with shaking hands and stared at the few words inside which stated that I would be granted my diploma when I finished my courses. I wished that I could have shown her a real diploma and hadn't forced her to make do with having to pretend. She was proud of me anyway.

"You will finish, won't you?" she asked.

"Yes, Mom. I promise."

Three months after she died, I wrote the final exams and essays and I got A's in both courses. She would have been truly proud if she had known that. That was the first of many things that she would never know.

After the ceremony, she gave me a gold pendant, an eternity knot with a diamond in the centre. Two years later, I lost it. I still did not care enough about myself to care for the things that I treasured or for signs that others treasured me. I would learn.

While the other families milled around the square, my father and I stood awkwardly beside my mother's chair. They wanted to meet my teachers and my classmates. My mother always looked forward to such social occasions and handled them graciously. But this time she kept having to vomit. It was another way in which the cancer was eating away at her dignity. As the other families held picnics on the grass, we had no picnic. We pushed my mother past the family groups to the nearest of the metal barrels that had been set up to collect the picnic rubbish and held my mother's head as she vomited. I think people avoided us, even though I tried to help my mother keep her dignity. Maybe we didn't belong there amidst the celebration of life. My mother, my father and I were experiencing another commencement. The beginning of a journey that was meant to be kept secret. There was no place for death on that sunny college square.

Soon after the ceremony, we had to catch a flight back East but in the frenzy of studying which had led up to the graduation, I had still not packed my clothes, books and other possessions. I spent two hours cramming things into trunks and boxes. It seemed as though the more I packed, the more there was left to pack. While my parents waited for me at the inn, the time of our flight got nearer. The more time I spent packing, the more stuff there was to pack. I had to leave some of it behind. Looking back, I suppose my failure to pack my things before that day was another attempt to delay death. I wanted to stop every day in its tracks and stop night from coming.

* * *

"Go have a bath," my mother murmured from the bed where she lay dying.

I had been caring for my mother for several weeks by this time and I was too tired to move, never mind bathe. I had been awake with her all night, soothing her, lifting her on and off the portable toilet, trying to help her with the pain.

"Come on now, take a bath," said my father.

"Too tired," I replied and started moving towards the kitchen to make more coffee. I heard whispers from the sickroom. My mother's urgent voice.

"You need a bath," she said again. "Your mother wants to talk to you," my father called.

I went to her. She was lying flat on the bed, too weak to move.

"You smell," she whispered.

I smelled. It was that animal stink again, that greasy, womanly stench from unspeakable parts, emanating from my armpits, from the creases beneath my breasts and from the folds between my legs. I was embarrassing her with my nature oozing from my pores despite my efforts to be a good daughter. The odour recounted a history and betrayed me to my mother.

I tried to be a good daughter as I cared for my mother during those last weeks. From the day I arrived home with her to Baltimore, she gradually became more and more dependent on me. Her dying was the birth process in reverse. I, who had been her newborn, became her mother. I slept lightly at night, half-listening for her cry. I bathed her, fed her and helped her to go to the toilet.

I used my tasks as acts of contrition that might purify me and earn me her forgiveness. With each servile prayer, I tried to wash away my guilt.

It was as exhausting as, I imagined, caring for a newborn might be. I had no time of my own. Every moment was taken up with caring. The difference was that in caring for a newborn one must feel a joy in the infant's growth that sustains the nurturing. With my dying mother there was no sustenance. Only irreversible decline and decay in our losing battle. I wanted it to end. I couldn't take anymore. But I had to stop it from ending because if it did, she would die.

I was constantly by her side trying to comfort her. We had never been so close and yet a reserve remained between us. We were not talking about the important things. We avoided our unfinished business. All the time a moment when we would finally talk dangled enticingly before us. There must be time, I thought.

I tried to summon the courage to talk to her once or twice

58

after I arrived home. In the beginning, when my mother was still lucid and seemed to retain at least some of her emotional resilience, there were things I wanted to say but was afraid to. I wanted to tell her the whole truth about the Professor. I wanted to talk to her about Clive. I wanted to tell her that I was sorry for so many things. I wanted to tell her that I couldn't imagine what it would be like to live without her. Even though we had lived at long distance for four years, she had always been at the other end of a phone line. Every time I had taken a risk, I had also taken it for granted that she would be there to support me if I fell. I wanted to tell her that I was afraid that I would not be able to survive without her and that I was appalled by what the cancer was doing to her body.

But I was a coward. I kept smiling. I played the cheerful nurse.

When I arrived home in Baltimore on the night of May fifth, our life seemed almost normal. Although there were little signs. During our flight home, my mother had been in excruciating pain. The ungenerous seat on the plane was too constricting for her and the seatbelt was cutting. She seemed terribly frightened, whereas in the past she would have negotiated airports and flights with aplomb.

Once home though, she seemed to revive. She was able to get out of bed in the morning and get dressed on her own as she always had. At midday, she liked to sit outside on the patio in the sun. She had a deep tan from sitting in the sun all during the spring.

"I love the sun," she said when she laid back on the chaise longue, letting her body relax with the heat.

Soon she will be in the dark. I had to stop myself from thinking. *No sun will reach that flesh*.

In the beginning, she could make her own way out to the sun and sat quietly dozing. I would bring her iced drinks that she couldn't swallow. The glass would sit by her chair until the ice was melted and the liquid had turned warm.

Later, when her movements became too painful for her to walk unassisted, Mark and I helped her to walk outside and recline in her chair. Each of us supported one side of her. She was so heavy that her legs could barely support her. We struggled under her dead weight. One day we let her fall. As

59

we lowered her onto the chaise longue, we lost our grip and she fell onto the chair. As it collapsed under her, she rolled onto her side on the ground, screaming in pain. I had never heard my mother scream before. I didn't know she had it in her to make such an animal cry. The twist and fall of her body had obviously wrenched her internal organs made tender by the cancer. We felt guilty and terrified that she would die from internal bleeding. We telephoned her doctor.

That evening, he came. He declined our invitations to sit down and to accept a cup of coffee. He stood by the living room sofa where my mother was lying, his car keys in one hand, and looked down at her sternly. He was much younger than she, in his late thirties. Already the brilliant doctor in the forefront of cancer treatment.

My mother looked up at him through her pain like a hurt child aching for some comfort.

"Pull yourself together," he said. "There is nothing more we can do for you now." He dismissed her pain as he had dismissed her life. She embarrassed him with her hanging around. She was his failure, after all. The woman who refused to die.

I tried to make him listen to me about what had happened in the garden when she fell and how she had cried out.

"I'm afraid she's damaged something," I told him.

He looked at me incredulously as though he thought I was exaggerating her pain. As though he thought I was stupid.

They asked me to leave them alone. The doctor talked quietly with my father and finally left behind a prescription for pills. My brother and I couldn't get the picture of my mother falling out of our minds. For my part, I kept seeing her grimacing in pain. I feared that by dropping her we had made the pain of her death worse. I suspected that we had hastened her death.

My mother stopped sitting in the sun. Most of the time, as the month of May ended and June began, she was quiet and uncomplaining as she lay in her reclining chair in the family room. She needed help to do ordinary things. A little more help every day. She refused to eat and so I searched the cookbooks for invalids' food, bland custards and broths. All she would take was protein drink in tiny sips. Just enough to make me a little less worried. She was on hunger strike, starving herself to death. An active fifty-two-year-old woman had become as feeble as a ninety-two-year-old. It was horrifying to see.

She gradually withdrew from the world. She even stopped watching TV, not that she watched much in the first place. She had always been too busy working and raising a family. The only time I ever saw her sit down was when she did her schoolwork in the evenings, correcting papers and writing little notes: "You can do better; very good; good work; or, keep trying harder, I'm proud of you." Sometimes, to be especially encouraging, she drew a little round face with a big smile to let the child see how pleased she was. When she wasn't correcting papers, she was working on her Master's Degree thesis or reading or doing laundry.

I was amazed to discover on my arrival home that she had developed an interest in the afternoon soap operas on TV, despite the fact that she has always ridiculed them in the past. I supposed that since she had been forced to take leave from her teaching job, soap operas had helped her to fill her the lonely afternoons of empty time.

When I watched them with her, the larger-than-life characters with their parody of suffering distracted us from our genuine tragedy. Then one afternoon my mother suddenly lost interest.

"Turn it off," she said.

I complained.

"Please, turn it off," she asked again.

We didn't watch any more soaps operas after that. It took me a while to figure out why. My mother would never know how the plotlines developed. She would never know whether or not the kidnapped girl would be rescued by her ex-husband or whether or not the gentle, old doctor was really a drug dealer.

Those absurd characters with their false lamentations would live on and my mother would not.

During the first few weeks at home, while my mother dozed in her reclining chair, I sat on the sofa nearby and played with dice. Over and over again I rolled the dice, hoping each time for a higher score, bargaining with fate. The dice clattered

61

onto the glass table top. The rattling sound promised hope. It was numbingly addictive.

My brothers were there, too, but each of us was silent in our own worlds.

My mother perked up for visitors, too proud to let them see her at her worst. The young pastor from the local church that my mother attended on Sundays visited and prayed with her. (My father had become a church administrator at that time.)

"She's an amazing woman," the young pastor told me. "She has great faith."

I was glad to learn that she had some solace in her belief that she would be resurrected into eternal life.

Her friends stopped by too. I wanted to ask them to help me but I didn't know what to ask for. They were kind but they always looked so relieved to be leaving. Our pain was not part of their worlds. On their way out the door, they inevitably said, "give us a call if there is anything we can do." There was nothing anyone could do.

I couldn't impose death on them. I was in the death world. They were not. When my mother's friend, Mona, called to say she was coming to visit I hoped that she would give me a break from the constant caring. Maybe give me some advice. But five minutes after she arrived, I found Mona hiding upstairs in the hallway, weeping. I put my arms around her and comforted her. I understood why she was so shocked to see my mother's sickly yellow death mask. I had grown used to it. Death did not make me cry anymore. Death was my medium and I moved in it like a snake moved in water.

I also realised that the banal rituals of dying were too intimate to share with outsiders. I didn't need help. I was learning how to care for my mother as I went along. I had never known death and so every lesson took me by surprise. I never expected that I would have the responsibility of easing someone into death, so in the constant fight to halt death's assault on my mother's dignity, I improvised.

Drinking water from a glass, for instance, hurt her throat too much so I gave her water from an eyedropper, drop by drop. She twisted her head away.

"Mom, please take a little. You're going to dehydrate."

She pursed her mouth shut. No food, no water, how was

she staying alive?

Bathing, too, hurt her because she couldn't move very much. For the first few weeks, I helped her lower herself into the bath and I stayed with her because she was afraid that something might happen. She loved her baths. I filled the tub with steamy, hot water and with my mother's sweet-smelling bath salts that created a creamy foam along the surface of the water. She lay in the water with her eyes half-closed and spread a facecloth modestly over her bosom, hiding her breast and her scar. The bubbles from her bath salts covered everything else and she reminded me of a movie still I once saw of Doris Day looking simultaneously prim and naked amongst the bubbles.

Once, my mother had invited me to look at her scar where her breast had been.

"You see? It's not too bad," she said. I knew that she was showing it to me, because she didn't want me to be afraid in case it ever happened to me but I was so frightened that I could only make myself glimpse at her scar. I wondered, could she see my apprehension? Did it make her feel worse?

Eventually, my mother was in too much pain to move in and out of the bathtub. So I tried again to improvise and I bathed her using the shower spray as she sat in a plastic garden chair in the bathtub. She made me stop. She was hypersensitive and the spray of warm water hurt too much. And maybe she was too shy to let me see her so brazenly nude in the chair. I curtailed the bathing operation and returned her to her bed.

I felt ashamed that I hadn't perceived her modesty right away. I was immodest, I supposed.

Instead I bathed her in her bed with a warm cloth, keeping her covered over with sheets and towels so that I did not embarrass her.

It was too late to improvise an intimacy as my mother lay in bed uncomplaining, her face stoical against the pain and the disappointment. In one sense we had never been more intimate and yet everything we should have been talking about was left unsaid and we continued to suffer in our ordinary way, proudly concealing our feelings from each other like many mothers and daughters do.

I was still too afraid of upsetting her to talk to her honestly and I was sure she felt the same way about confronting me so that the loose ends of our relationship were unresolved and raw. I kept hoping that the caring would bring us close enough to talk. But as the cancer started to take her mind, making her distracted, we communicated in other ways. During the nights when my father was away, I tried to console her. When I heard her cry out, I crept into her bed and cradled her. Holding her fragile body in the dark and feeling her thin hand in my strong one, I prayed for a miracle. I tried to conjure up a healing power within me that would suck the cancer out and leave my mother whole. I tried the laying on of hands. I even offered myself in her place. My guilt was my most terrible burden.

One day, I was looking through a closet and I found two new blue suitcases, unused. They were the suitcases my mother had bought when she was planning to visit me in Europe. It was to have been the trip of a lifetime, and I had not let her come.

My mother had always wanted to see Europe but she had never been able to afford it. Her children's education was her priority so that all my parents' money was taken up by the tuition for private schools, colleges and universities.

During the year that I was living in Paris, she discovered that it would soon be too late. A close friend who knew of my mother's situation gave her an airline ticket and some cash so that she could visit me. My mother got her first passport, bought the new suitcases and started packing.

But I told her not to come. I was afraid that she would be uncomfortable in the cold, damp fourth floor flat I was sharing with Clive. And he refused to move out long enough for her to stay there for a week. He said she should stay in a hotel. I tried to explain that she could not afford that but he still refused to cooperate.

So I gave my mother an excuse. My flat was too small and cold, I told her. I told her that I was roughing it and that unless she could afford a comfortable hotel, she wouldn't enjoy Paris. In truth, I was still hiding my life from her. Maybe she knew that.

For years afterwards, it killed me to imagine her in a public office in Baltimore, excited to be applying for a passport for her first trip to Europe and unaware that she would never get a chance to use it. I imagined her asking the clerk if her new passport would get to her in time. I imagined her writing the cheque to pay the fee and having a short conversation with the clerk in which she told him that she was going to visit her daughter.

I didn't know then that if she didn't visit Europe immediately she would never see it. I wished that she had told me that. I wished that I had been in a better situation so that I could have had the joy of showing my mother Paris. She would have loved the museums and the cafes.

My shame at refusing her visit is so deep that I can still remember it only with tears. My mother had her own regrets about her life and shared them with me, sparing me none of her pain. She was only fifty-two. She hadn't enough time to fulfill her dreams. I listened to her confessions and tried to comfort her. During those final days, my mother's remorse and mine mingled easily. We were the one regret, mother and daughter.

There was no comforting possible because she wanted so much to live. During her four-year battle against cancer, she had continued to deny herself as she always had so that she could pay for our college education. Maybe she should have sold our summer house and quit her teaching job a year earlier and spent the year travelling in Europe. It must have crossed her mind. Instead, as she told me, she wanted to leave it to her children. Yet suddenly, with her life gone and she not ready to lose it, were these choices right? She told me that she wished she had been able to be selfish and to put herself first, at least sometimes. All her life she had put her children first and postponed her own needs as though she had plenty of time, like other women her age. She looked forward to retiring early and travelling as soon as her children had finished college, leaving her with more time and money.

As for my future, that was as hard to talk about as hers. I told her, "Mom, I'm going to be alright."

"I know," she said. "I know."

I'm not certain she was convinced. Would I be alright in her terms or mine? She wanted me to get rid of Clive and to find

65

someone worthy of me, although she never said it in so many words. Most of all, she wanted me to have a career. She thought I should be a journalist. To me, this seemed an unattainable prospect.

Our awkward attempts to discuss this business were hampered by the fact that the future was not a point of reference in those final weeks. We moved from minute to minute, hour to hour, expecting nothing from time except sorrow. Yet at the same time, I continued to hope and even believe that she would rise like Lazarus. Despair and hope existed as the one emotion. I could see no hard evidence that she was going to die. I had never seen anyone die before. I didn't know what to expect. An objective eye would have seen the inevitable signs: the constant vomiting, the yellowish skin, the swelling abdomen. But part of me believed that a miracle was still possible.

"I'm going to be okay," she kept saying, "I'm getting better."

Her entire abdomen was distended, as large and as taut as an eight-months-pregnant woman's. She looked like this when she gave birth to me, I thought. Now she is giving birth to death.

"I know, Mom. You're going to be alright," I said. I helped her fight off death. I believed with her that she would live. To believe in death would have been disloyal. I continued to play the role I had adopted of cheery, business-like nurse. I helped her dress in her prettiest clothes. I stood her in front of her full-length mirror and said, "don't you look great?"

She started to weep and sat down at her desk.

"Come on, Mom, it's okay."

"Leave me alone for a while," she said.

"Mom, are you alright?"

"I need to be alone."

I left her sifting through a pile of papers at her antique, cherrywood secretaire that the parishioners of my father's first church had given her. She could hardly sit up. She was trying to get her affairs in order. I had heard the phrase. Until then it had only been a phrase.

My mother had in front of her a lifetime of letters, documents, bills, photographs. Years passed before I had the

66

courage to look through these things. Eventually I looked and found a neat pile of letters written on blue airmail paper, from me to her, the year I lived in Europe. I forced myself to read them and wept at how false and arrogant I was, offering nothing but dropped names and unimportant details. Everything except how I was really feeling. Those letters were an insult, they only fooled her for so long.

In the final weeks, she spent many hours sorting through her belongings. I couldn't bear to watch how carefully she handled them, her hands so weak that she could hardly hold things and her movements as tenuous and slow as an old woman's.

She left her things neatly arranged, ready to be found. She left her combs and eyeglasses and make-up and jewellery, all practically placed as though she would wake up one morning soon and get dressed again. She left her clothes in immaculate condition. Did she think about what would happen to her clothes?

When she was gone, I buried my face in her clothes so that I could smell her. I inhaled the spice of her perfume and when I sank down onto the floor of her closet, I smelled the warm leathery scent of her shoes and the stale odour of stored winter clothing. When I rested my head against her winter coat, I was sure it still smelled like snow. This was also the cold smell of mothballs and hide-and-seek and of Christmas presents hidden on the high shelf. I wept for her clothes. They were my goodbyes: to smell her clothes and finger through the memories.

As I helped her to die, I didn't want to think about what would happen to her things. After many years, my father would eventually give her clothes away to charity. After that, I imagined that someday I might be driving down a street in Baltimore and see a proud, black woman wearing one of my mother's dresses, a navy one. The dress would shout to me: "Remember?" It would sing my mother's song, but not only hers. Above my mother's alto, this strong woman would have added the flourish of an extravagantly crimson, soprano hat, covered with large, hungry-looking poppies. My mother's dress would nearly burst with the vigour of this stranger-woman's syrupy walk as she marched down the street, scolding her well-dressed children. She would be walking to church. The dress would command its place in the front pew, filled to shaking with the woman's soprano vibrations.

Death recycles clothes, earth, pain, anything.

As my mother fumbled through her bureau drawers, I still didn't know that she was leaving things for me to find afterwards, things that I would never be able to throw away. There were the unintentional keepsakes, the combs, brushes, a pillbox, pins, cheap jewellry that I gave her when I was small. They were things that I would carry in my handbag for years, gradually losing them, dispersing them, like dust.

I would also find the metal lozenge box containing two pale, dry wisps of hair. They were our first curls, mine and my brother's. I would keep them for her in my own bureau drawer. They would continue to remind me that once I was the child my mother prayed for, a perfect being. The wisps would tell me of the times that she and I were totally in love and spent hours staring into each other's eyes, smiling at each other. How were we to know what would happen to us?

It was her way of telling me, after she was gone, that such decaying curls and other things must be kept as memorials to childhood. All children died and left behind the shells of adults too concerned with things that didn't matter. The two blond curls contained my childhood optimism and imagination and reminded me of how much my mother nurtured these qualities because she loved me. And as I grew older, the curls in the tin box would become even more the texture of my mother's hair as she lay in her own, deep, silent box.

She also left for me some baby clothes, handknitted sweaters and caps, a tiny, treasured nightgown. I would keep these, too, in a room which waited to be planted with a child. I would imagine my mother, when she was dying, holding those clothes in her hands and envisioning the day when she might have become a grandmother. I would imagine what might have been, myself complete and delighted with my newborn and my mother coming to visit me in hospital, carrying a package and inside, carefully wrapped, would be those small clothes.

"These were yours," she might have said as she laid them on the bed before sweeping her grandchild up into her arms.

That would never happen.

I would not find everything she left. Somewhere hidden, would remain a christening dress and my mother's wedding dress. I would not try to find them for fear I might fall apart.

She told me, as she lay half-awake in her bed, that she would leave behind one thing more important than all the others, a legacy that would keep her presence with me and my two brothers for the rest of our lives. It would be the beach cottage in Chatham on Cape Cod where we would continue to go in the summers to remember her. The cottage was the place my mother most loved to be. She grew up in New England and living south, in Baltimore, had always been her compromise. My brothers and I agreed after she died that we wanted her to be buried at Chatham so that she would always be close to us, always alive in our happy childhood memories of that place.

My mother would never know her grandchildren, but they would play in the water where she swam and feel the same sand between their toes. In those future summers which she could only imagine, the cottage would be our grandmother, embracing us.

Two weeks before my mother died, in mid-June, we brought her to Chatham. Maybe it made sense that she would die in a place she loved. Maybe we just couldn't bear the thought that she wouldn't see another summer. She had already sent my two brothers to Chatham earlier and they found their usual summer jobs to earn money for college. It was important to my mother to know that my brothers were on course, doing what they would have been doing anyway.

The day we left Baltimore, the doctor gave my father pills for my mother to take. They were supposed to knock her out and make the journey more comfortable for her and, maybe, ease her trauma at knowing that she would never go back there again.

I felt her intense grief but I also knew that she was strong and that she hated feeling "out of control". I wanted her to have the dignity of saying goodbye to the house, which was filled with her beautiful things. Against my father's wishes, I didn't give her the pills. After we dressed and packed, I helped her down the stairs, then assisted her into her wheelchair and started to push her out the door. She let me know, silently almost, that she wasn't ready. She gestured with her head to show me where to push her.

She wanted to say goodbye to her house. I wheeled her slowly from room to room and watched her absorb the memories of the home that she would never see again. We stopped and looked at the dining room as though we were examining the exhibits in a museum. She was calm as she looked at the beautiful, handmade, early American cherrywood dining room table, chairs and sideboard which she had carefully chosen as a bride. Inside, there were her silver pieces and the hand-engraved crystal given to her by her father's parishioners on her wedding day, twenty-six years earlier, almost to the day.

I tried to help my parents celebrate their anniversary, but they hadn't the heart.

We toured the living room and my mother took one last look at the colours she had chosen and at the furniture and pictures she had arranged. I watched her savour these last moments. I tried desperately not to fall apart. My mother remained composed, bestowing on her home a reverence which I had seen only once before when I was a child and an old Japanese woman, dressed in a kimono, visited our house. My mother asked me to show the bent old woman our garden and so I brought her outside, expecting her to stroll casually through it. Unexpectedly, the old woman walked slowly and delicately as though she was afraid of breaking the grass. She stopped before each rosebush and bowed, closing her eyes in silent prayer.

I had never known such pain as my mother's goodbyes mustered. Whenever I felt that grief could run no deeper, grief cut another swathe like a river tearing at its banks. My Aunt Ruth and her eldest son, David drove to Baltimore in a camper van to help us bring my mother the five hundred miles to Chatham. So many times my aunt had driven all night with her children from their home in Rhode Island to be with us in Baltimore for Thanksgiving. Aunt Ruth's arrival always brought wonderful times. None of us had imagined then that one day we would be making this awful journey.

There was a bed for my mother in the camper so that she

could sleep most of the way. My father, Aunt Ruth, David and I didn't talk much during the nine-hour drive to the Cape. I felt exhausted and pressured and couldn't articulate what I was feeling. I have to be strong, I kept thinking. I tried not to think about all the other drives to the Cape in the month of June when we had been buoyed up by the promise of summer.

At the Cape, my mother worsened quickly yet continued to insist that she would recover. At least, I think that's what she meant when she said, "I'll be fine." Maybe she meant that she would be fine in the afterlife. I wish I knew.

My mother remained tenacious and would not let death take her. So it satisfied itself with other things for a while, first the bed. My father and brothers dismantled it and stored it away in the attic. A delivery truck brought a rented, steel hospital bed that could be tilted, raised and lowered. I hated it.

"She will be more comfortable," my father said.

"Yes," I thought. "This means she really is going to die." Then, a second later I told myself, "don't let yourself think that. Don't let her die."

But it wore me down. I began to see her death as a release, even though I felt selfish and ashamed to think it. Her pain continued to be unmanageable. Her bloody throat could no longer swallow the doctor's pills. She complained that it was like swallowing rocks. I was sure that it was, for I had held the red-stained tissues to her mouth while she coughed up bloody scraps of her lungs.

I continued to invent ways to help her. My father crushed the pills and mixed them with applesauce in the hope that she would swallow them. He telephoned her doctor and a community nurse arrived with a bottle of morphine and a hypodermic needle. The nurse told me that I would have to give my mother the injections myself when she needed them. But how would I know when she needed them? I'd know, the nurse said. She demonstrated how to do the injection on an orange.

She made me plunge the needle into the bright, juicy fruit in the same way that I was supposed to plunge it into the soft muscle of my mother's upper thigh. When I told the nurse that I could do it, I believed that I could.

71

But I couldn't. The needle terrified me. I was afraid that I would cause my mother pain when I stuck it into her or worse, that I might kill her if I allowed an air bubble into the needle's chamber. I was afraid that the morphine would cause her to go mad and turn her into a drug addict and that she would lose her dignity and not be our mother anymore. So we kept trying with the pills.

I didn't know then that more than a decade later, I would still hate myself for not having the courage to use that needle. I would know that she should have had the morphine and that she need not have suffered. I would know that there should not have been such pain.

But in those last days, how was I to know? I had not met death before and there was no one who could clue us in. People visited. They made small-talk. Then they returned to the living world. I couldn't blame them. What was happening to my mother was very difficult to accept.

Just as the visitors instinctively withdrew, my mother continued to withdraw from the world. We brought her to the beach one evening at sunset when the ocean and sky shimmered in shades of pink, gold, lavender and blue. She had taken so many early morning walks on that sand, seen her children grow up there, taught us to swim there. We couldn't bring her wheelchair onto the sand and she turned away.

"Take me home," she said. She didn't want to say goodbye.

When my mother's sisters and brothers arrived one afternoon from Rhode Island, I could see that they were shocked at my mother's appearance. My mother asked me to help her sit up in her wheelchair. She hadn't sat in it since the evening we brought her to the beach because it was too uncomfortable for her, yet she wanted her family to see her at her best. She didn't want them to know. So I dressed her and my father helped me lift her into the chair. She put on a good act. She even laughed a little. My aunts and uncles chatted with her and told stories about the old days in Pontiac, Rhode Island. Those stories, the treats of my childhood. They distracted me for a while and my mother, half-asleep, seemed to let their visit wash over her. I could tell she was following only parts of the conversation.

Their visit reminded us all of the days we spent together

when my mother and her brothers and sisters were younger and had their children around them, chasing each other on the beach.

When I looked at my mother's ravaged face that day, I saw her youthful face. The face that I had believed would live forever.

I don't think that my aunts and uncles knew that they were saying goodbye. My mother kept the upper hand. She let them go believing that they would see her again. She wanted to demand nothing of them. She wanted to cause no trouble.

Before she left, she told them, "Kathy is taking care of me. She's such a good daughter."

A few days later, we would phone them to say that my mother was going into hospital. They would dash to their cars and drive the 120 miles from their homes to the hospital as fast as they could but they would arrive at the hospital to find that we had gone home. That is how they would find out that my mother was gone. My aunt would say, "We didn't know she was so sick." We did a good job hiding death, all of us.

How much pain my mother felt nearing the end, I don't know. She concealed it and refused to complain when she could not swallow the pills anymore. I suspected that she had resigned herself to the pain.

My father kept asking her, "Is the pain bad? Do you need something?" But my mother didn't reply. It seemed like her mind was going. We phoned the nurse again but she was too busy to come outside her scheduled times. I tried to ask my mother again, "Do you need more for the pain?", but then I realised that she had lost her voice. Her throat was too decayed for her to speak.

We tried to interpret her sounds, my father and my brothers and I. We were like the parents of a sick infant who couldn't tell us what was wrong.

One evening she started to cry out.

"Way-ay E-ee. Way-ay E-ee," she cried.

"What is she saying? we asked each other. We listened, trying to decipher the message.

"Worried? What are you worried about?" my father asked gently.

"No..." my mother seemed to say, shaking her head and

73

squinching up her eyes. Then again, she repeated her cry. "Way-ay E-ee. Way-ay E-ee."

We guessed dozens of words. It seemed to last hours.

"I have no idea, Dad," I said.

She strained to lift her head to make herself heard.

Again, she cried, "Way-ay E-ee." Her message seemed urgent, literally a matter of life or death, yet we couldn't make sense of it.

She laid her head back on the pillow and wept, then fell back into the coma-like sleep that had overcome her in recent days.

After a while, she reawakened and started to plead with us yet again, "Way-ay E-ee. Way-ay E-ee."

My father took off his glasses and put his face close to hers. He looked into her eyes. "What is it?" he asked.

"Way-ay E-ee."

It was only after her funeral that I finally realised what she had been trying to say. Going through her things on her dressing table, I found her wedding ring.

"Wedding ring," she had been saying, unable to pronounce the words because of her swollen and bloody mouth and throat. She had wanted to be buried with her wedding ring. I realised then, a day or two after she had died, that she had finally accepted her death.

But I was also angry that no one had told us about the ring. There should have been an etiquette to ease death. There should have been a community around us to remind us of the traditions we were too distracted to research. Even the people at the funeral home didn't bother to ask if she would have wanted to wear her wedding ring. We were so isolated.

As I write this, I am holding her wedding ring which my father gave to me. I keep it in a box on my dressing table and so many times I have wished that I could open her grave and put it on her finger. I wish I could do it now.

The last days of June, 1980

As my mother's death approached, I began to panic. When she died, I would not know how to mourn. Where were the women who would wash the body and lay it out for the family to sit with and pray for throughout that first night of death? Where were the women whose keening would give us permission to cry? All I would be offered would be valium and comfort from people who would be afraid to catch my eye but would try to make me laugh, meaning well.

I began to realise that all my life I had been protected from death yet it had been with me all the time. Death was removed from life and neatly packaged in white hospital rooms. We kept the bodies safely away from us, cloaked in the pretentious decor of the coffin and the funeral home in order that we might remain protected. I had been so much a part of this communal deception that even in the seconds before Mom's last breath, I still wouldn't know what death was. Until my mother died, I would have not a hint of how the loss would make me feel.

As she clung to her last hours of life, I asked myself: what is it like to die? What transformation takes place?

Are you watching over me, Mother? Or are you dust?

I remembered her telling me, when I was a child, that her own parents visited us from time to time, in their way. They were spirits, she said, who could pass through us unnoticed and observe our lives.

"One of them may be sitting in that chair right now watching us but we will never know," she told me.

She described for me the death of her father, the Swedish pastor, whose spirit was seen by her mother to rise up from his body. This, I took as solid evidence although later, when I started questioning the existence of God, I wondered if it was merely a soothing fantasy, imagined by my distraught grandmother to ease her anguish at her husband's passing.

75

My mother was a long time dying but it was only in those final hours that I began to loose strength. During her final two weeks, she slipped in and out of a deep, coma-like sleep. As the end approached, her sleeps grew longer and deeper. During the final days, we tried to rouse her from unconsciousness, terrified that she would never awaken.

My father called her name, "Ardis, Ardis." She responded to his voice and when she opened her eyes, her face took on a beatific expression, like an infant staring into the eyes of its mother.

My father called me in to see. She looked into his eyes with a pure and forgiving love as though they had never argued or disappointed each other, their loose ends instantly resolved.

I continued to clutch my unfinished business to my heart, aching to tell her what I had always been afraid to say. *Please understand, mother, what he did to me I could not stop. It sent me on a journey to places I wish I had never gone. I know I disappointed and frightened you. I am sorry, most heartily sorry.*

A day or two before she died, we had been unable to awaken her for nearly twenty-four hours. In terror and despair, I knelt by her bed and cautiously lay my head beside her breast, careful not to hurt her.

"I love you, Mom," I told her, believing that she did not hear and wondering if this would be the last time I would say those words while she lived.

Every time, as death approached, was the last time: the last time she would hear me say I loved her, the last time I would kiss her cheek, the last time I would bathe her, the last time I would feel warmth in her hand, the last time I would hear her voice.

Then, for the first time, I said what I had been afraid to say for so long.

"Mom, I don't want you to die."

It was the first time that I had despaired in her presence. It was the first time I had surrendered my role as the strong nurse who could deal with anything. It was the first time I had admitted in her presence that she was going to die. I had tried to remain inscrutable against death because I had been afraid to let her see my pain, believing that it would ease her anguish to see me behaving stoically. It was foolish of me to hide my feelings.

76

If I were dying, I realise now, I would want to see the painful tears of loss on the faces of those I loved. Did I deprive her of my grief? (I seem to have no shortage of memories that evoke the most excruciating guilt.)

With my knees on the floor and my arms around my mother, I breathed in the smell of her like the tired child that I was.

All my regrets about my relationship with her and about my own behaviour crowded into my head. Why hadn't we been able to talk? Why, always, was there a distance between us, a fear of candour? I could not tell her the truth about my life for fear that I would make her miserable. And the things that did come out of my mother's deep-rooted and repressed anger, near the end, came too late to be resolved. I felt powerless to heal her and overwhelmed by the tragedy of her life.

She was dying too young. She felt cheated and angry. My contribution to her unfinished life had been enormous. I was an extension of her. She would live on in me and yet she detested my moral choices. Later I would understand my mistakes but I would never have the chance to explain to her why I made the decisions that had upset her. Children rebel. That's healthy. With maturity, they usually reconcile with their parents and while the generations may continue to disagree, they may at least reach some understanding of why they are different. My mother and I never had that chance. She was denied the fulfillment of seeing her daughter blossom. With her death, I lost my chance of ever becoming the prodigal daughter.

I realised all this a decade after her death. But as I leaned against her death bed that day, I was confused and remorseful.

I wanted to be her daughter again. I realised too late that I needed to rely on her support and comfort. I wanted her to know how much I hurt, but cloaked in the darkness of her final slumber, it seemed that she would never know.

Then, gently, I was roused from my dark contemplation by her hand lightly stroking my head, comforting me. She delicately caressed the nape of my neck with her cool fingers in the same movement she used to lull me to sleep when I was a child.

She still loved me. Perhaps, even, she forgave me. No

longer the wayward twenty-three-year-old daughter, I was miraculously the child again in the embrace of its mother. I felt momentarily purified by her touch, as by a blessing.

Raising herself out of her coma was the first of many ways my mother would make herself felt to me during the mourning years.

Her death opened a door to the spiritual world that exists parallel to our own. I was surprised, and yet not, when my mother's father appeared to her in her bedroom shortly before she died. I did not see him myself, but I have no doubt that he was there. I was sitting beside her bed, trying to drip some water into her dry, cankered mouth from the tiny eye-dropper. She was drifting in and out of a profound sleep. She lay back on the pillow, exhausted, with her eyes half-opened.

Suddenly she became alert. Her face brightened and was animated with happiness. Her gaze was directed towards the end of her bed. The expression of sheer joy in her face was utterly hopeful and innocent, again like a child's.

"Daddy," she said.

Her voice was raspy, but the word was clear enough.

I looked at the end of the bed, at the chest of drawers against the opposite wall, at the ceiling, at the floor but this mundane scene offered no evidence. I looked back at my mother's expectant face and into her eyes which were bright after having appeared milky and dead over the previous days.

"What do you see?" I asked.

"Who is it?" asked my father. He was smiling and seemed not at all surprised by what was happening.

She ignored us. We watched her face.

"Daddy," she said again.

From that moment on, I felt him with us. So I stopped expecting to see him like some Hollywood ghost and looked instead into my heart where I could see, quite clearly, my grandfather who had died before I was born.

The way my mother timed her death was the second sign that during her final lapse into coma, she remained aware of us. The day before she died, her breathing suddenly became laboured and blocked due to a build-up of fluid in her lungs.

"The death rattle," my father said.

The words were brutal, but there was no other description

for that terrifying gurgling, wheezing, clattering noise made by her breathing. For the first time in my life, I became frightened of my mother. Death had invisibly infiltrated our house and it was hanging over her bed like a guillotine ready to cut her off from life. In my eyes it had changed her from a gentle woman into a Medusa. Several times a day she needed to be washed and her sheets and nightgown changed. I began to touch her with a new terror because I expected her body to undergo some monstrous transformation wrought by death, which could come at any moment. I was frightened at the prospect of of how she might look in death's embrace.

The trauma I had experienced of being unable to effectively control her pain had made me feel even more helpless against death. When the "death rattle" began, my panic increased with her every strangled breath. We had wanted her to die at home but when my father suggested that we call an ambulance to take her to hospital, I agreed. If I had possessed faith in my own ability to care for her as she passed away, we would have kept her in her own bed at home but we were worn down by our anguish, and hers. We had struggled to negotiate a battlefield of emotions in a losing war.

As soon as the paramedics arrived I was sorry that we had called them. Instead of offering her hospice and a gentle death, they immediately started to intervene. I rode with her in the back of the ambulance down route 6 to the hospital in Hyannis, twenty miles away. The ambulance roared down the centre of the highway, scattering cars to either side, while a paramedic worked on my mother, forcing a tube down her throat to clear her lungs. She writhed in protest. It was torture for her to have the metal-tipped plastic tube shoved down her raw throat which had been rotted by cancer. It was torture to watch.

"Do you have to do that?" I shouted above the siren.

"She's in a critical condition," the ambulance man shouted back at me accusingly. "She has cancer. We know she is dying," I said.

"It's our duty to do everything for her that we can," he replied coldly, as though I wanted her to die.

Hadn't we been doing everything for her that we could? In the emergency room, we waited with my mother for a long time. She was lying on an uncomfortable trolley. Being moved by the paramedics from her bed at home to a stretcher and now onto the trolley had obviously twisted her cancerous abdomen in some way that caused her enormous pain. For the first time during her illness, she moaned and cried in her agony. We kept trying to get someone's attention. I don't know why, but I had brought the morphine and the needle in my purse. I wanted to use it.

A young intern finally came to examine her and he ordered that she be X-rayed.

"Why?" we asked.

"Hospital procedure", was the reply.

My father and I sat helplessly in the hallway outside the room in which she was to be X-rayed. Then the real hell began. We heard my mother screaming in pain as they moved her from the trolley to the X-ray table. She wept desperately.

"I have the morphine in my bag," I said to my father.

"Maybe we should give her an overdose," he said. Euthanasia had never occured to me. Now it seemed the only way to stop the hospital torture. We hadn't the courage.

Finally, after a few hours spent diagnosing the obvious, the doctors admitted my mother to a quiet, private room. A nurse injected her with something for pain, which we were grateful for (and I'm sure my mother was, too) but when the death rattle began again, the nurse insisted on suctioning the fluid out with a tube stuck down my mother's raw throat. My mother's eyes were wide with an animal panic and fear as she fought the nurse.

"Do they have to do that to her?" my brother asked. "She hates it."

"It's hurting her," I said to the nurse.

It had to be done. It was hospital procedure.

Finally, they left us alone with her. We silently sat around her bed until evening. I silently prayed for that eleventh hour miracle.

We did not know how long she would last and thought that it might be a few days so we decided to sit with her in shifts. My father and Stephen would remain with her until four o'clock in the morning and then Mark and I would relieve them. At home that night, neither Mark nor I could sleep. I wrote in my diary that night of my overwhelming desire to have a child. Giving life, carrying it within me, was the only anecdote to the dance with death that I had been through with my mother. I believed that giving birth would heal me by balancing death in my life. Only birth could fill the deficit of strength and hope and desire that death had caused.

Mark and I returned to the hospital and sat with my mother through the morning while my father and Stephen went home for a rest. I watched idiotic game shows on a tiny television that hung from a crane over my mother's bed. Mark didn't watch them and I was aware that watching TV might be disrespectful but I needed to numb my mind and, I suppose, I was a coward.

As my mother lay comatose she soiled the sheets several times. Each time, I helped the nurse to clean her and to change the sheets. Mid-morning, a new shift of nurses came on with a different attitude about this. After my mother again soiled herself, I pressed the button which signalled the nurses' station that we needed help. An older nurse arrived, a redhead with a hard face. I asked her if she would please help me clean my mother and change the sheets.

"We like to wait and clean them when they're gone," she said.

Then she left the room.

Her callousness knocked me cold for a few moments, then I became enraged. I demanded to see someone from hospital administration and then complained to them at the disgusting and insensitive way the nurse had responded to our request.

I was in tears and, maybe, as I was railing against the nurse's behaviour, I was really protesting against death.

The administration sent a nurse to remain with us full-time.

I told her what had happened. My brother and I were enraged.

"You must be very careful what you say in front of your mother," she said quietly. "It is possible that she can still hear us. We think hearing is the last to go."

Again, I felt deflated. I had failed once more. Nobody tells you anything about death, I thought. For every person, must there be this wicked game of search and discovery? When you are caring for someone you love who is dying, do you have to learn from your mistakes? There isn't enough time to make mistakes. These errors leave lasting scars.

After the nurse told us that, Mark and I started talking to our mother, telling her how much we loved her. Telling her that we didn't want to lose her but that we would be okay.

My brother held her hand gently. He and my mother had been so close and much more intimate than she and I had been in our constant struggle to understand each other.

Late morning, the nurse took my mother's blood pressure which was dropping rapidly.

"It'll be soon now," she said. "I think you should call your father."

I phoned him and we waited for him to arrive. My mothers' eyes were wide open and unblinking.

"Her eyes must hurt. They must be dry," I said to the nurse.

She put a square of damp gauze over each eye to keep them moist. It also protected us from having to watch those horror-struck eyes.

While we waited for my father and Steve to arrive, I had an overwhelming need to see the babies in the hospital nursery, thinking naively that I could use the sight of life to counterbalance death. I was being melodramatic again. When I found the nursery, there was only one infant there and its skull, its two legs and its two arms were in casts. So much for my attempt to orchestrate a happy ending, I thought.

I returned to my mother's room but I must have been away longer than I had thought. Mark was waiting for me in the hallway. He and Stephen had been looking for me. My mother was about to leave us any minute and they were afraid I would miss her death. We went into the room and circled her bed, holding hands: my father, his mother, my two brothers and myself. While my father prayed aloud, I closed my eyes and wept. Then one of my brothers whispered my name and I opened my eyes and looked at my mother. She was heaving her last sigh. Her chest was slowly sinking into the bed, expelling more air than I thought possible.

"Whoosh-sh-sh-sh," her breath went, so quietly. Her body gently pushed life out. And that was it. She simply stopped breathing. It was finished.

She had waited for me, I was certain, so that we would all

be together around her when she left us. That was the second sign for me that there was something beyond death. Perhaps the separation between her body and her soul had already begun and she was able to consciously let go.

I hoped that her timing of her death meant that she had finally accepted that she was going to die and that her death was not merely the arbitrarily-timed breakdown of her central nervous system, rotted away by cancer.

As we stood around her body, I was afraid to look at her staring eyes, now dead and still hidden by the two white patches of gauze which I had kept moistened throughout the morning. Maybe we all were. I do not know how long we stood around the bed for time had stopped. I was holding her tapered hand, finer and more elegant than my chubby paw and trying to memorise the way it looked. I catalogued the almond-shaped fingernails, the faint lines across the back of her hand which was still brown from the weeks she spent sitting in the sun before she died. Her hand was bare, youthful. It hadn't dawned on me yet that she was without her wedding ring.

Holding her hand, I felt the life drain out of her so quickly, much faster than I would have imagined. Within minutes, she was being transformed from my mother into a corpse. The skin on her thin, sun-speckled arm suddenly lost its tautness and became flaccid. Her entire body seemed to shrink a few inches, sinking lower into the bed as her life-force drifted away. The body was just a body. Without its life-pulse, it wasn't my mother any more.

I tried to see her spirit rise but I could not. All I felt was emptiness, a loss more profound than I had thought possible and I could think of nothing but her permanent absence from my life.

I looked up and saw my father weeping and Stephen trying to comfort him. I don't remember that my brothers and I cried.

I don't remember us ever crying in front of each other after she died. Each of us had our private grief and we never shared our feelings together. Our joint loss was intuitive and bound us together. Although I cannot speak for them, I know that from that moment on, I remained arrested by the trauma of her death for many years to come.

We left her in the hands of the nurses. It wasn't satisfactory at all. The tradition of family members bathing the body and dressing it in its shroud died out long ago. Still, I wanted to do this for her. This was the body that had given me life and, to me, it was still sacred. People have told me since that cleansing one's own dead is a beautiful and powerfully therapeutic experience. But then, I only knew this as an outdated, possibly barbaric custom. Death would be taken out of our hands and the rituals would be performed by people who were paid to do it, professionals with no emotional stake in the process. At the time, I felt intuitively that having cared for her intimately for months, I was not properly finishing my duties by leaving her in the hands of others. I dared not speak about the handling of her corpse for fear that it would simply be seen as another sign of my eccentricity. We left her in the hands of the nurses. My father said that the hospital staff would handle her with respect although, after the performance of that unfeeling nurse earlier in the day, I doubted it. I kept my thoughts to myself. After we left her room and had closed the door, Stephen went back alone. He wanted a solitary moment with her, I guessed. I admired his courage.

I have never asked him what he did when he went back, but I have wondered whether or not he did what I hadn't the courage to do, which was to remove the squares of white gauze and, tenderly, close her eyes. Someday, perhaps, I will ask him.

We drove home along route six, the same road on which the ambulance had raced less then twenty-four hours earlier to bring my mother to the hospital. I watched the people passing by in their fast cars and I felt, again, a distance from the world as though I was not a body at all but a mere soul. How could the world go on as before when we had just lost our mother? How could people look at us and talk to us as though nothing had happened?

We passed a skidmark where my mother and I had nearly been killed the summer previously. She had been driving when an enormous truck travelling in the opposite direction crossed the double-yellow line and came bearing down on us, head-on.

My mother froze. The truck was coming at us at sixty miles per hour at least. I shouted to her, "Turn it to the right," then I reached over and grabbed the steering wheel, pulling us into the ditch, just in time. We weren't out of danger yet, we were headed straight for a metal roadside barrier and my mother managed to steer us clear, I don't know how. Behind us cars crashed together with the splintering, crushing sound of metal and glass. We sat shaking, knowing that we had come within seconds of certain death. My mother began to weep, which was understandable after such a shock. When we got home, however, her crying only worsened. I had never seen her so despairing. It was as though we had really been killed and we had become ghosts, mourning ourselves. It was not until the moment that we passed the same place on the road, an hour or two after she died, that I fully understood her pain the previous summer. She had been mourning her own death. Death had reached out and touched her and reminded her that she should have been taken already. I didn't understand then that the doctor had already given her a death sentence. I didn't know that she was truly keening for herself.

Her pain filled me that first night of her death. I was too numb to feel my own.

I fell asleep with the help of half a valium tablet that night and the next. I felt empty and exhausted and bruised. I was filled with her absence. On the third night, after her funeral, my mother made her presence felt to me again. I half-awoke, deeply aware of her presence. I began to feel myself floating, surrounded by a warmth that was precisely the same temperature as my body. It is difficult to describe the sensation, which was like nothing I had ever felt before or have felt since. It must have been what a foetus feels like, floating in the womb. I felt completely calm and at peace and I had the sensation of my body being completely supported on all sides by a firm pressure, as though suspended in a viscous fluid. I felt like I was being completely embraced in every molecule of my physical and spiritual self by some benevolent energy.

There were two beds in my bedroom and I was sleeping in one, my mother's youngest sister, Helen, in the other. Suddenly, my aunt rose and kneeled on her bed, holding her arms out towards something above my body and shouting my mother's name. My aunt had not seen my mother in years because she lived far away and she had flown to the Cape for my mother's funeral the day after she died. She shouted my mother's name in agony. It sounded as if she was trying to stop my mother from walking off the edge of a cliff.

I realised, next morning, that I had experienced my mother's final goodbye during the night. The feeling of being suspended in warmth was simple to explain. My mother had bathed me in pure love. I thought of the stories I had heard, told by people who were revived after being clinically dead. Their stories were always the same. On the brink of crossing to the land of the dead, they had been greeted by a being of light which emanated pure love and offered to escort them to the next dimension.

Are you there, mother, a being of light, waiting for me?

My father said that it was possible that the dead experienced the trauma of separation as keenly as the living. Maybe that explained the unsettling feeling my brothers and I had all that summer of my mother's presence. We kept expecting her to walk into the room at any moment. When the telephone rang, we expected it to be her. Once, my brother thought he saw her looking in on us through the glass door to the patio.

"It will get better with time," an old friend of my mother's told me at her funeral. It does not get better. I still ache for her. I needed her when I was lost and had no one to turn to. I needed her the day my husband was diagnosed as having cancer. I needed her when I got pregnant and lost the baby.

I couldn't cry at her funeral. I can cry now. Sometimes I think that I have spent the past decade trying to remain in control and that I am only beginning to mourn.

I have learned that death is not a single moment. It is ongoing and exists in that eternal present where love also remains rooted, long after the lovers have parted. The pain of my mother's death is always fresh when I remember how much I need her.

There have been so many things I have wanted to talk to her about. Sometimes, when something wonderful or terrible has happened, I have said to myself, "I must phone Mom and tell her." There is a part of me where she is not dead.

Sometimes, in my imagination, we have conversations. I have asked her, when you lost your first pregnancy, mother, did you become anxious and depressed for months, like I did? Did you blame yourself, too?

We never had a chance to have those womanly conversations, those hours spent at the kitchen table ruminating ruthlessly over the details, analysing and embroidering upon events and emotions, stitching them together into a patchwork quilt of patterns that make sense. Other women have served in her place, offering love and talk, but you know what they say about a mother's love. It is irreplaceable.

The fourth sign of her presence, after death, came during the quiet, dark summer nights after the funeral, when my father, my brothers and I were sitting in the living room in Chatham with the windows and doors open. After nightfall, one of us noticed the singing of a lone bird.

It seemed to be coming from a tree near the kitchen door. None of us could identify the type of bird (we were city people). Its song was sad and distinctive and it continued always in the black of night, all summer long, coming from the same place. We could never see it, only hear it, and it never sang during the day. One of my aunts said that when the birds sing at night, it is a sign that Armageddon is near. But we heard only one bird and we believed it was my mother.

When she was gone, I kept thinking, *she will never know how her story ended.*

I felt paralysed in the moment of her death, unable to move on to the next stage. When I tried to cry, the tears would not come. When I tried to write, the pages remained blank.

My brothers still had university to structure their lives. I was supposed to be going out into the world, finding a career and making my own way. I tried life in New York, got an apartment and a place in New York University film school as a graduate student, but the city weighed down on me. I couldn't grasp life there and I spent too much time hiding in my apartment, afraid to go out onto the street. I had no self-confidence and no energy. When I did go out, I came back sweating and exhausted. I tried to order my life with food, with lack of food, with alcohol, with lack of alcohol, with a boyfriend, with the lack of a boyfriend.

I found the same inertia in Boston. The problem wasn't the city, it was myself. I tried Dublin and worked heartlessly on my master's degree at Trinity College. Inside, I felt dead. Mere survival was enough.

And then, after four years of this depression, I started to get out of my self-imposed isolation and write free-lance journalism. I met a young magazine editor. We had coffee together. He blasted my head clear with his brazen enthusiasm and wit.

"This job is just to get me through," he announced one day over coffee. "I'm going to be a novelist and when I'm in my forties, I'm going to make films." I believed him. It was an act of faith. And he laughed a lot when I talked. He thought I was classy and funny and asked me why I wore such old-fashioned clothes.

We stayed up all night talking, snuggling together under his duvet, both of us fully clothed in two jumpers each. He did not want what was not being confidently given. My mother would have liked him.

I had a dream in which I saw his face and I said to him: "You magical man, I'll love you for forty years."

A few days later, he asked me to marry him. If I didn't marry him immediately, he said, he would have to cut himself out of my life. He couldn't bear to be with me and not be married to me.

There was only one thing I could do.

That is how I was rescued. Ferdia stole me away and married me but to him marriage didn't mean that I was supposed to get up in the morning and cook him breakfast. He had married, so to speak, my potential and he set about nurturing me and encouraging me to develop my talents. We were so deeply content with each other that we were convinced that my mother had a hand in it. There were so many coincidences along the path to our meeting. We felt that each of us had been led to the other.

It was as though neither of us could blossom without the other. He saw abilities in me that I had failed to recognise and he constantly pushed me, refusing to let me hide in being a housewife. He helped me to become what my mother had wanted me to be, a journalist. He coddled me along on those first frightening steps until I could run by myself. We were happy, astonishingly happy, then the dream turned into a nightmare. A year after our marriage, he collapsed at a dinner party. He lay on the floor, unconscious, with his eyes open and staring. I thought he was dead. His blank, surprised, unseeing and unblinking eyes looked like my mother's eyes as she lay dying in her coma. Blood was streaming out of his ear and spilling into a red pool on the floor beside his head.

"Ferdia," I kept shouting his name. The world had come to an end again. He was dead. The man who had saved me and loved me more than I had thought possible was dead. My mother was taken, now Ferdia. It wasn't fair.

"Ferdia." I think I was screaming. His eyes stared up at me, unseeing and unresponsive. He was really dead. While I telephoned for an ambulance, a friend kept pounding on Ferdia's chest, trying to administer coronary pulmonary resuscitation. He managed to rouse Ferdia and to make him sit up. Ferdia started vomiting blood. I put my arm around him. He shrugged me off.

"Who are you?" he asked me.

In the ambulance, I sat beside him holding onto his arm and supporting him so that he could stay upright. I was afraid he would inhale his own vomit if he lay down.

The ambulancemen thought that Ferdia was drunk. He kept pushing me away rudely as though I was nothing more than a bothersome woman who had found him lying on the street and was fussing over him for her own gratification. This was the ending of our life together. It would never be the same again. In the accident and emergency room, he lay raving on a trolley, trying but unable to get up. When I tried to talk to him, he dismissed me utterly. This man who had insisted that I marry him after knowing me for one week, still didn't recognise me.

The bleeding on the surface of his brain, the extradural hematoma, had struck like lightning. We felt relieved, when it was over believing, like others struck by lightning, that it wouldn't strike twice. For six months, Ferdia and I moved like strangers around each other. He was utterly changed. Once vibrant, he had become morose and withdrawn. In the spring, we moved from our damp, cold, dark basement flat to a warmer, brighter, modern apartment which lifted our spirits. Then, in the summer, nearly a year after the bleeding on his brain, Ferdia began to be himself again. There was a little lump in his testicle, but only an infection, the doctor thought. We tried to get on with our lives.

By December the lump had become a painful, burning swelling and Ferdia was admitted to hospital. I began to relive the hours that I had spent with my mother, waiting to discover if her breast lump was malignant. The day of Ferdia's biopsy, I remained at home by the telephone. Hospital corridors were soul-destroying places to hang around, I had learned. I spent those tense hours re-potting my plants, giving their roots fresh, nurturing soil and room to grow, which was, looking back on it, just what Ferdia and I needed.

The telephone never rang. Instead, our GP came to our apartment.

"It's not good," he said.

I started to cry.

"You'll have to be strong. You might have to live with this thing for ten years," he said.

Inside, I screamed at God and wrung His neck. I wasn't going to be able to survive this. This wasn't a broken leg, it was a long, drawn-out, death sentence: the benevolent despot again, coming back to torture me. After the years of uncertainty created by my mother's cancer, followed by that four-year depression, didn't I deserve a little happiness? A life with cancer hanging over you was not a life, I told myself. It was a charade pretending to be life. I was not getting the life I deserved, the life that everyone else seemed to be able to take for granted.

I believed that real life meant having the luxury of living under the illusion that it was going to last forever and if not forever, at least indefinitely. I wanted to love my husband and have a family with him, knowing that our love would last for forty years and that we would see our children grow up.

When testicular cancer was diagnosed, we stopped being mere lovers. We sacrificed our intimacy to being strong for each other. I found myself playing the role of carer again, just as I had with my mother, supporting Ferdia's hopes as fervently as he supported mine. Each of us was afraid to let the other see our tears. It took us years to realise that cancer had become a barrier between us, just as it had between my mother and me.

When my mother was diagnosed, I had to grow away from her to ensure my survival. I was at the age when it was natural and healthy to leave home and become independent, but because I had to do this while my mother was so sick, I felt like I was abandoning her. With Ferdia, it was the opposite. I clung to him even more closely and was even afraid for him to leave the apartment on his own, I was so terrified of what might befall him. I believed for a long time that cancer made me love Ferdia even more. The truth was that cancer made me afraid to love him. To be completely and intimately trusting of him would have been to open myself to an even greater hurt. I couldn't admit to myself that, just as I had grown away from my mother, I was growing away from my husband.

I became more independent of him knowing that if I was, it would be easier for me to survive if he died. In many ways, it was healthy for me to take on more responsibility and to have to summon the self-discipline to handle the stresses of my job in *The Irish Times* as well as caring for Ferdia, although it was even worse for him, continuing his own newspaper job while also undergoing chemotherapy at the weekends. The fact that he could do that inspired me to keep going yet often, when I was working evening shifts in the newsroom, I felt like I was abandoning him. I thought of him home alone in front of the TV and I wanted to be there with him to bolster him up and to cook him a good dinner. We conserved our energies exclusively for each other when we were not working and had very little social life. We felt isolated because few people our age shared our concerns. They were buying houses and cars and having babies and having fun. We were like old people, obsessed with surviving the threat of death. Although I was never tempted to have an affair, for a while I could understand why the husbands and wives of people who develop life-threatening cancers sometimes turn to affairs for comfort. Such frightened people want a healthy lover so that they can hang onto the illusion that they will be loved forever and never abandoned.

It took a long time for me to realise that cancer and the fear of loss were the reality behind the illusion and that by seeing the puppets' strings, so to speak, I wasn't being short-changed.

Hope, I learned, depended like the theatre on the willing suspension of disbelief. Until I understood that, I hated God. The chances of Ferdia being stricken with either an extradural haemotoma or cancer in at his age were miniscule; the chances of getting both were practically unheard of. Why was God doing this to us? It was a sick joke. I began to believe that I was doomed to love people who would get cancer and die.

We lived one day at a time. I kept my job going, alright, but Ferdia was my main preoccupation. I had to keep him alive, keep him strong and optimistic. My mother, in the dignified way she coped with her cancer, had taught me to be brave and just when I believed that I had not one shred of energy left to cope, I found more strength. She was always there.

Ferdia was almost impossibly positive, refusing to give up. That made it easier to handle the dread, but he had to learn to cry, too.

Every morning when I woke up, I felt normal for a split second, then the fear would inevitably spill into my consciousness: "Ferdia has cancer. He could die, not today, maybe not in six months' time, but before, long before, his time." The adrenalin would start pumping and the alarm bells would go off in my head. The day and I would grapple with each other, like two weary fighters, our arms around each other's necks, too tired to win, too tired to lose.

I was overburdened with the unfairness of it all. God, with a little help from my mother, had given me the man whom I loved and who loved me more than I thought it was possible to love anyone and I was losing it all. During the four years in which I had kept my hopes up for my mother, I had believed with all my heart that she would live. I despaired of keeping my hopes alive with Ferdia. I couldn't be part of this grand deception anymore. There was no point in believing that life was anything but black because I was bound to be disappointed in the end, anyway. I felt like Sisyphus, pushing the boulder up the hill only to have it roll down the other side so that I had to put my shoulder to it once again and push it up that hill, eternally.

Beneath it all, I had a nagging ache deep inside that told me I deserved what I was getting. My life was blighted because there was something wrong with me. This knowledge was not something I articulated, it was just there, throbbing, telling me these things were my fault.

We made it through. When I woke up in the mornings and felt that I could not go on, it was my mother who kept pushing me to keep going and told me to keep loving. The night that Ferdia nearly died, when his immune system collapsed as a result of the chemotherapy, the medical staff worked hard to save him but I knew that it was my mother who watched over him, protecting him.

Later, she kept protecting us when we were recovering from the trauma of the cancer. Ferdia and I experienced a bad patch in our relationship as we tried to readjust our relationship away from being carer and patient, back to being lovers again.

The answer came from my mother then, who said, "forgive". Once we had learned that, there was no looking back.

We didn't worry about the future anymore. We lived in the present. I stopped wanting to believe in the illusion that life would have a happy ending and started learning to take joy in those moments when Ferdia and I were snuggling under our duvet, contented in each other.

When I die, I want to be wrapped up like that with Ferdia in a space capsule and sent into orbit eternally.

We grew accustomed to a tolerable level of uncertainty. There was the gradually diminishing fear that Ferdia's cancer would come back but alongside it, growing in urgency, was our fear that we would never have children. We were told when Ferdia was diagnosed as having testicular cancer that it was unlikely that we would be able to have children. At first, we were just glad that his cancer could be cured. Then, when our lives began to get back to normal, the realisation that we may not be a family brought on a second depression worse than the first. We had something that we could not cure: dashed hopes. But we got used to it.

We stopped being selfish and no longer demanded one hundred per cent of everything from the world. We told ourselves that we would make the most of what we had. When childlessness made me sad, I told myself that having children was not all it promised to be. I relished my friends' horror stories about sleepless nights with squalling infants.

Still, the fear of cancer returned occasionally to nag at me and I began to remember my mother's warning to me that I had a far higher than usual risk of getting breast cancer myself because hers had occured premenopausally, which meant that it was most likely to be a type with a genetic risk factor.

It is a game, playing with hope, that each of us will one day lose.

"You know you're going to lose," my husband said, "So you might as well enjoy it while it lasts."

Sometimes I am glad that I have learned the lesson at thirty-four instead of at sixty-four.

Two years after Ferdia's cancer was diagnosed, I became pregnant, by a miracle we felt. Three weeks, four, I felt it growing. Four weeks, five, six, I could feel my body swelling with the promise of a new life. Ten weeks, twelve, my jeans didn't fit anymore. I believed in life again, genuinely. The world seemed full of hope. At twelve-and-a-half weeks, I bled.

God couldn't be doing this to us again, I thought, tearing away what he has given.

I went for an abdominal scan. I sat in the waiting room, my bladder painfully swollen with the litre of water I had been told to drink. My appointment was for eleven, we waited until noon.

"This is water torture," I joked to Ferdia who was waiting beside me, trying to be cheerful. It was going to be alright. The pregnancy handbook said that some brown spotting was normal. Soon we would be seeing our baby on the monitor. After waiting an hour, I was brought into the scanning room.

"Can you see the screen, dear?" asked the radiologist.

I could.

He pushed a plastic wand against my abdomen, making soft craters in my flesh. I watched the monitor, afraid to show how excited I was to be getting my first look at our baby. "How many weeks pregnant did you say you were?"

"Twelve".

"Did the doctor confirm that you were twelve weeks pregnant?"

"Yes."

"You had a pregnancy test?"

"Yes, three."

"If you are pregnant, it is very, very early."

Of course I am pregnant, I thought. Three tests. A visit to the obstetrician/gynaecologist. A lecture from him on the evils of weight gain. An internal examination. My breasts prodded and poked. Everything "normal".

I lifted my head so that I could see the monitor better. All I could see was a nonsense of fuzzy black-and white contours like a view of the surface of the moon. My baby is there among those shapes, I kept thinking, it has to be.

When we were children, we watched the first moon landing on a black-and-white TV set at our beach house, which was hundreds of miles away from the nearest transmitter, which meant that our television reception was very poor and we hardly ever watched it. One day my mother told us all to stay home from the beach. We were going to see the moon on TV.

My mother excitedly described the historic images on the television set, which to us were unintelligible.

"See that's his foot. He is stepping down from the ladder now. Look, he's the first man on the moon. He is putting his foot on the moon," she said.

We squinted at the blurry images and tried to make the rapidly moving dots on the screen come together into a picture of astronaut Neil Armstrong in his space suit.

"My parents would have been amazed to see this," my mother said. "They never would have believed it. And when I am gone, you will see things that I never would have believed."

This gave the fuzzy image on the screen new importance. We moved closer to the screen.

"He is bouncing, do you see?" my mother said. "That's because he's weightless. There's no gravity on the moon."

I wanted to see my weightless baby, floating in my gravity-less chamber, moving me that one small step to being healed.

"One small step for mankind," my mother repeated. We could just about see an indistinct white shape, bobbing on a background of grey.

The radiologist turned the screen away. He said something to the nurse.

Then he said to me, "I am going to tell your doctor that if you are pregnant, it is too early to tell."

"I don't understand."

"Your doctor will explain."

"I thought I saw something there," I said.

The radiologist pointed to a black crescent, the shape of Neil Armstrong's moon.

"That is your womb."

Surely, that was a foetus, that lunar curve.

"It appears to be empty," the radiologist said.

Later, the obstetrician/gynaecologist explained. "You have an empty sac. It is really what we call a blighted ovum."

Blighted, like potatoes or wheat.

"You'll be having a spontaneous abortion," he said.

I started to sob and once it started, I couldn't stop it. The tears were as stringent and overpowering as the ones my mother wept the day we were nearly killed. The grief flowed out of me in great lumps of water.

I had allowed myself to be deceived again. I had believed in life when, in fact, there was no life there. There had to be something wrong with me.

The doctor was speaking. My husband was nodding and holding my hand. The doctor stood up. He straightened his pristine white cuff. He fiddled with his cufflink. He was sorry, but it was time to go. Full waiting room outside. My husband helped me to stand up. I walked with him and I wept and for a long time, we sat in the car, unable to believe it. I had never known such tears.

Then it emerged, over months, growing inside me. That throbbing core of self-hatred, subsumed all those years ago, began to fill me up and burst its way to the surface.

The scene with the Professor started playing in my head over and over again, especially when my husband and I made love.

When I wept for my lost baby, I wept for myself in that room, for that naive, nineteen-year-old girl, wanting to be a concert pianist and giving it all up, giving in. And for the first time I remembered my thoughts as I left the Professor's room and walked from the conservatory out to the park, to sit on the bench.

No young man will ever want me now. I will never get married and have a family. My mother said that two people make love when they care so much for each other that they want to give themselves to each other and become one. I cannot give what has already been taken.

I was filled with a knowledge that I did not want to consciously admit and which gradually forced its way into my consciousness until it became undeniable. I did not deserve a child. It made sense that I lost the baby. A depression so severe hit me that I felt I couldn't cope anymore. Ordinary days left me shattered. I began to weep, to shudder, at the slightest things. It was as though I had anaesthetised myself against a pain so deep, that I forgot it was there. And now, years later, the anaesthesia was wearing off and exposing raw nerves.

I started having dreams about my baby, who was withering

away because I forgot to feed it. I left it alone for days on end to starve. Then, two years after the miscarriage, I dreamed my baby was not a baby at all but a slug as black and slimy as blight. In one dream, I was sitting in an auditorium with thousands of people. I was in the front row, waiting for the houselights to come down and the stage curtains to open. The tumour-black slug fell out of me onto the floor. As I watched it wriggling, it turned into a tiny, green alligator. I wanted to kill it. I kicked it and it didn't respond; it just kept growing. I tried to stab it with my twelve-inch long, thin, razor-sharp knife but I made no wound.

The serpent was resilient and its spongy skin repelled my attacks. I stabbed it again and it merely grew larger. Its fresh green colour began to turn green-black as the sea and its soft, spongy skin started to grow hard scales. I was terrified that it would soon grow large enough to kill me. I wanted to run away but I couldn't stand up. Then, as I watched mesmerised, the creature transformed itself into a baby, wriggling in a blanket on the floor.

"That's your baby," the man sitting beside me said.

"That's not my baby," I told him. I walked away and hid in the back of the auditorium. "That baby is not mine," I kept thinking, "I don't want a damaged baby.

Then I realised what I had done, "Oh God, why did I damage that beautiful, perfect baby?"

I found myself sitting with the people in the back row, staring at the floor. A blond, happy, baby boy came toddling towards me, smiling. He was one-year-old and gorgeous.

"This is your child," said a woman standing behind the baby, pushing him towards me.

"He's not mine," I informed her.

The child was so beautiful. But he must have been brain-damaged by my attacks, I thought. I noticed that his eyes looked intelligent. I could see that there was nothing wrong with him despite all the damage that I caused him when he was just a tiny alligator.

The woman said, "If you don't want him, I'll take him."

When I woke up, I was thinking, "I will never have a child. I am not the mothering type."

Then, I wrote my mother a letter. I spared no details. I told her all my secrets and, most importantly, I told her of my guilt.

I had another dream. I was with my mother and she was smiling at me. Her face was elfin and very young and she glowed with energy. I was amazed too see that she was pert and girlish, much younger than me. She didn't walk, she skated, flipped, flew. She hovered in the air, beckoning me to follow her.

You can be whatever you want to be.

She didn't say say these words, she infused me with them. They bubbled up from my deepest spring. Then I had a knowledge, in the dream, that someday I would have a child. It was an inarguable fact. My mother and I were joyful together, like two children playing. We had no history, no guilt, no future.

We just are.

I woke up the next morning feeling calm and happy and more rested than in years.

For ten years I had wanted to reach her so that I could ask her to forgive me. At last she was telling me, *forgive yourself.*

Epilogue

When my two brothers and I were children, my mother used to show us the stars. On summer nights at our beach house, we would wrap up together in an enormous blanket and sit out on the porch for hours, staring up into eternity. We were small enough then for all three of us to snuggle with my mother inside one enormous blanket on one enormous deck chair, with our heads poking out and our necks bent backwards so that we could see the black sky and the handfuls of stars thrown carelessly against the dark. My mother would tell us, again and again, because we asked her to, how the stars were older than the world. She would tell us how they were here before us and before our parents and our grandparents, whom we had never known, and before our great-grand-parents, who had lived in Sweden, and long before them. The stars were older than the world and they would be here long after we were gone. Many of them, she explained, were only light travelling towards us faster than we could imagine. They were not stars, but the light memories of stars that had died long ago, each leaving behind a sparkling pinprick to mark the place where it had been. That pinprick of light, made millions of years ago, would keep travelling towards us for millions of years hence, long after we ourselves had stopped travelling.

We asked her where the blackness and the stars ended and she replied that space was infinite, like time. And I tried to imagine infinity going back and back before the world was created, when it was still, my mother said, a thought in the mind of God, who had existed even before that.

"When will the world end?" we asked my mother.

"No one knows," she said, "But even when the world ends, time and space will continue forever, into infinity."

"Will we be here for infinity?" we asked her.

"Everything must end," she said. "But when people die, we believe they exist in infinity."

"What is it like?" we asked her.

"No one knows. All we know is that everything in the world keeps changing."

I felt so warm and comfortable and safe beneath the blanket, where my brothers and I lay half-asleep, snug against each other.

"I want this to last forever," I said. "I want us always to be here the way we are right now."

My mother was quiet for a while and then she said, "you will not always want to be here with us. Someday, other people will matter to you more. You will have your own family and you will want to be with them."

I could not imagine wanting to be with anyone except my family or wanting to be anywhere except on that porch, beneath the murmuring shadows of pine trees, looking past their branches into the stars.

I am not yet a mother, but if someday I become one, I will be like my own mother, providing security for my children by letting them believe, as long as it is possible, in their own immortality. And I will let them believe, as long as believing is possible, that I will never leave them. And when they leave me, I will rejoice in their independence and pray that no harm comes to them. But first, when they are small, I will be most like my mother. I will believe that I am able to express in myself the parts of her that were most positive, while suppressing, or better, transforming the negative to suit my newly discovered self. I will believe that I can do that, but in truth, I will be more like her than I can possibly imagine now. And my child, because my child is like me, will be like my mother too. And in the moment when my child and I, each stubborn in ourselves, stand off before each other, each holding onto our own pain, my mother will sit unseen in a kitchen chair, laughing. My child will not see her but will think it hears a bird singing outside the kitchen door. And I will laugh with my mother and hug my child and say, "Oh, how your grandmother would have loved you."

In later years, if it turns out that my child and I do not understand each other and keep to the habit of guarding our secrets protectively, I will know, just as my mother knew, that someday we three will meet together in a place where all is bountifully forgiven and where our secrets do not matter very much.